THE GENERATION DRIVEN CHURCH

Evangelizing Boomers, Busters, and Millennials

WILLIAM BENKE
&
LE ETTA BENKE

THE
PILGRIM
PRESS
Cleveland

The Pilgrim Press
700 Prospect Avenue East
Cleveland, Ohio 44115-1100
www.pilgrimpress.com

Printed in the United States of America on acid-free paper

07   06   05   04   03   02   5   4   3   2   1

Library of Congress Cataloging-in-Publication Data

Benke, William, 1927-
  The generation driven church : evangelizing boomers, busters, and millennials /
William Benke & Le Etta Benke.
    p. cm.
  Includes bibliographical references.
  ISBN 0-8298-1509-0 (pbk. : alk. paper)
  1. Evangelistic work – United States. 2. Baby boom generation – Religious life.
3. Generation X – Religious life. I. Benke, Le Etta. II. Title.

BV3793 .B46
269'.2 – dc21

                                                                2002072106

CONTENTS

PREFACE

THIS BOOK IS WRITTEN PRIMARILY with small to midsize churches in mind. Small is defined here as having a weekly attendance of under two hundred, and midsize as from two hundred to about five hundred. These represent the great majority of the churches in America today — probably between 85 and 90 percent of the total. Many are an endangered species in an era when big is often considered better and, more importantly, because it is a time of unprecedented cultural change. Most small and many midsize churches are traditional and have a one-size-fits-all ministry approach. Unfortunately, at least for tradition oriented churches, a majority of America's population has become nontraditional. That is, they have become largely postmodernist in philosophical outlook.

According to this perspective, there are no absolutes; relativism reigns; Christianity does not have a lock on spiritual truth; the community determines what is truth, right, wrong, and best for those within its group; subjectivism replaces objective thought, human reason, and empiricism; or to put it bluntly, anything goes! The Baby Boomer generation is largely postmodern oriented, and the Baby Buster generation (Generation X) that follows is almost entirely indoctrinated in a postmodernist mind-set. Together these two generations constitute almost three-fourths of America's adult population. If Generation Y, the Youth generation, which is also largely postmodernist oriented, is included, then over three-fourths of those above age twelve are postmodernist in outlook. Most postmodernists describe themselves as "spiritual seekers" but reject the traditional church as being out of date, out of touch, irrelevant, intolerant, conformist, and just one among many religious belief systems that have something positive to offer but none of which is the source of universal truth or divine revelation. Religious pluralism best describes most postmodernists in terms of religious orientation.

These generational differences translate into a new cultural paradigm. Add to this the distinctly different life experiences that have shaped each of the adult generations that compose today's society — Pre-Boomers,

Boomers, and Busters (Generation X) — and the result is three very different cultures, each of which requires a different ministry approach in order for outreach to be effective. Generation Y, as they move into adult status, will add a fourth cultural category. Unfortunately, many traditional small and midsize churches have not yet accepted or adapted to this reality. As a consequence, significant numbers are dying off and being replaced by new start-up generation driven churches that are structured to reach out to unchurched members of the Boomer and Buster generations using new approaches and methods to present the Christian message.

This book is a synopsis of the cultural changes that have brought us to where we are, the reasons for the changes, the characteristics of each of the generational categories mentioned together with related implications for ministry, and several alternative strategies available to traditional churches of small to midsize to help in refocusing their ministries to include an effective expanded outreach. Most traditional churches are inward focused, in contrast to outward or outreach focused. They minister to the Christian culture but are virtually devoid of conversion growth because of the absence of any meaningful outreach to the masses of unchurched adults that compose the postmodernist cultures. Continuing along this course is a formula for stagnation, decline, and ultimate demise.

The background information leading to proposed strategies has been gleaned from those who are well respected and recognized for their work and knowledge in the areas of postmodernism, church growth, and ministries to children, youth, Boomers, and Busters. A synthesis of such information and findings, this book offers an overview perspective designed to help update tradition-oriented church leaders concerning this new cultural paradigm and its implications for ministry. The strategies provided can translate the challenge into a new ministry opportunity.

The authors are management specialists in strategic planning and organizational problem solving and have been called upon to render organizational, management, and strategic planning assistance to a wide range of nonprofit and civic organizations, including churches. They bring a back-to-the-basics discipline in addressing the disparity between theoretical purposes and ministry realities that characterize most small to midsize churches today. Their analysis highlights the relative absence of conversion growth or evangelism taking place in these churches, even though universally acknowledged as one of the church's primary purposes — the reason for which the church exists. The approach used in addressing this issue — defining the problem, gathering relevant facts, identifying and assessing alternative solutions — constitutes an objective analytical report on the declining spiritual relevance of small to midsize churches in America today and what can be done to reverse this trend. Described are five alternative strategy models that provide the potential for changing tradition-oriented churches from a focus that is predominantly inward oriented to one that embodies a strong outward component.

Although the book is written largely from an evangelical Christian perspective, the characteristics that describe each of the several generational categories that make up today's populace are relevant and applicable to all Christian organizations, whether they are evangelical, mainline Protestant, Catholic, or parachurch. These characteristics describe today's "market," regardless of doctrinal persuasion, and must be properly understood and accommodated by all such organizations if they are to fulfill successfully their goals in this new cultural paradigm.

Chapter one

THE GENERATION DRIVEN TREND

THE CHURCH TODAY is entering uncharted waters. For the first time in human history we live in a generation based multicultural society. That is, the four major generational categories, other than children, that constitute today's society — youth (also referred to as Generation Y or the Millennial generation), Generation X (also called Baby Busters or the 13th generation), the Baby Boomers, and the Pre-Boomers — each represents a uniquely different cultural orientation. Children are not included as a component of this generation based cultural diversity since they have not yet acquired a "cultural set," that is, readily definable cultural values and characteristics.

Society has always been made up of several generational categories: children, youth, young adults, middle-aged adults, and seniors. In the past, the church accommodated these multiple generations with the traditional church programming to which older Christians have become accustomed. While such programming took into account age-related differences and needs, particularly concerning children and youth, ministries to the several adult generations were structured on the premise of relative cultural homogeneity, regardless of age bracket. The multigenerational aspect of church ministries or programs is therefore not new. What is new is that the transfer of basic core values and cultural traditions from one generation to the next took a sharp detour when the Baby Boomers entered the scene and were influential in launching the postmodern era. In the case of earlier generations, basic core values largely transcended age and provided for a certain cultural continuity. While younger generations have always displayed a skepticism toward the traditional and a tendency to explore new ideas, certain basic cultural underpinnings ultimately prevailed in terms of society as a whole. That multigenerational cultural continuity is no longer intact.

Figure 1-1 on the following page illustrates this discontinuity conceptually. In an earlier era (upper chart), unique cultural characteristics (represented by the horizontal arrows) existed for each of the four

Figure 1-1

PAST GENERATIONS

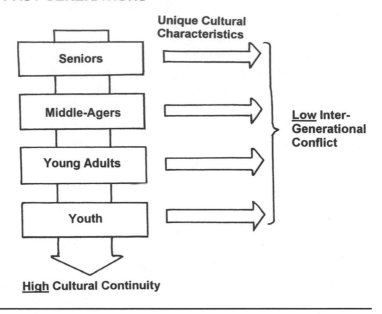

Unique Cultural Characteristics

Seniors

Middle-Agers

Young Adults

Youth

Low Inter-Generational Conflict

High Cultural Continuity

TODAY'S GENERATIONS

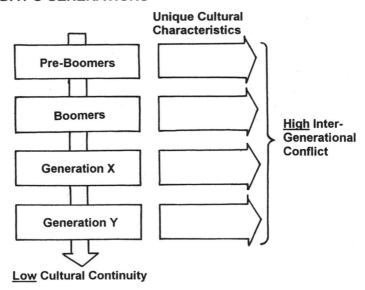

Unique Cultural Characteristics

Pre-Boomers

Boomers

Generation X

Generation Y

High Inter-Generational Conflict

Low Cultural Continuity

generational categories shown, but they were minor in comparison to the high level of cultural continuity (represented by the vertical arrow) as basic values were passed on from generation to generation. The result was low intergenerational conflict. In today's environment (lower chart), the unique cultural characteristics for each generation are significant, while the transfer of basic values from one generation to the next has greatly diminished. Each generational category has undergone unique life experiences and developed its own cultural characteristics, translating into low cultural continuity and high intergenerational conflict.

American society is now in a unique period of generation based multiculturalism as it transitions to this new cultural paradigm called postmodernism, the subject of chapter 2. Leading to this generation based multiculturalism has been not only the adoption of postmodernist philosophy but also the disruptive societal changes that have occurred as a result and that have impacted the several generational categories in different ways.

Birth dates specify today's generational groups: children: 1989–94; Generation Y, or youth: 1981–88; Generation X: 1965–80; Baby Boomers: 1945–64; and Pre-Boomers: prior to 1945. This last category, the Pre-Boomers, is sometimes divided into several subcategories, such as the Builders (born 1925–44) and Blazers or Seniors (born before 1925). Others use different terminology and divide them into GIs (born 1901–24) and Silents (born 1925–42). We have chosen to combine them into one category called Pre-Boomers. The approximate population distribution of these generational categories, along with the age range of each in the year 2001, is shown in the table on the following page.

The above delineation of generational categories by birth year is not universally accepted. Opinion seems to vary as to where the divisions occur. Neil Howe and Bill Strauss in *13th Gen: Abort, Retry, Ignore, Fail?* put youth, or the Millennial generation, at 1982 and beyond with no end date yet defined; Generation X at 1961–81; the Boomers at 1943–60; and Pre-Boomers at pre-1943.[1] We've elected to use the breakdown of Tim Celek and Dieter Zander, authors of *Inside the Soul of a New Generation*, whose breakdown matches many other writings on the subject.[2] However, regardless of where the age boundaries are drawn, there is broad agreement on the characteristics and related information concerning each generational category. If we exclude children and focus only on those

Generation	Year 2001 Age Range	% of Total
Babies/Infants	Below 7	10.0
Children	7–12	8.7
Gen. Y (Youth or Millennials)	13–20	11.5
Gen. X (Busters)	21–36	22.8
Baby Boomers	37–56	28.0
Pre-Boomers	57 and above	19.0
		100.0

Source: U.S. Census Bureau, 1998.[3]

beyond the age of twelve, the distribution by generational category is as shown in figure 1-2.

Note that Baby Boomers represent the largest segment at about 35 percent, followed closely by Generation Xers at about 28 percent. Together Generations X and Y represent about 42 percent of the total and are the population segments most influenced by postmodern philosophy, although Boomers are also influenced by certain aspects of postmodernism. Representing about 23 percent of the total population above age twelve, the Pre-Boomers are the segment most oriented toward cultural values prevalent prior to the postmodernist shift. The fact that the generational categories are now characterized by these distinctive names (Baby Boomers, Generation X or Baby Busters, etc.) tends to reinforce the contention that each is unique in terms of certain cultural characteristics. These differences and the resulting ministry implications concerning each are discussed in later chapters. The overall implication, however, is that in order for churches to remain relevant in this cultural transition period, it will be necessary for most to provide some combination of a modified approach, a much broader spectrum of ministries, or to target the generational categories to which they will primarily minister — the Pre-Boomers, Baby Boomers, or the Generation Xers. Regardless of which of these categories are targeted, ministries to youth (Generation Y) are necessarily included as well since, as minors, they are part of the households of these other generations.

Ideally, every church should have the broad spectrum of ministries necessary to accommodate all generational groups. Size and resource

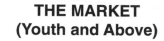

Figure 1-2

THE MARKET
(Youth and Above)

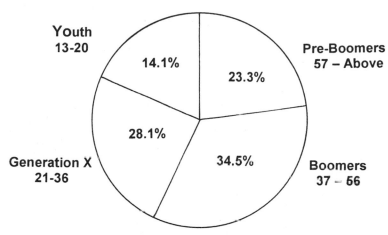

Youth
13-20

14.1%

23.3%

Pre-Boomers
57 – Above

28.1%

Generation X
21-36

34.5%

Boomers
37 – 66

(Age range shown is for the year 2001)

constraints, however, make this impractical or impossible for all but very large churches, which are relatively few in number. Most churches in America are small or midsized. According to George Barna about half of all Protestant churches in America have fewer than a hundred people in their congregations on a typical weekend.[4] About a quarter have two hundred to four hundred. The remaining 25 percent fall somewhere in between either the hundred to two hundred range or those with over four hundred in attendance. Fewer than 3 percent of our nation's churches have an attendance averaging a thousand or more each week. Accordingly, if the premise is correct that each of the generational groups mentioned has certain unique ministry needs, based upon their differing cultural characteristics, then it follows that the majority of churches in America will likely be unable to minister effectively to all generational categories by reason of size and resource constraints, as well as congregational intransigence that is also often a factor. The need for a selective generation driven approach to ministries, therefore, becomes increasingly evident for all but very large churches. Stated differently, there will be an ongoing trend toward churches that are focused in outreach toward selective generational groups, as opposed to a multigenerational orientation. This trend is already evident. Generation X churches are springing up throughout America to fulfill a need to which tradition-oriented churches, particularly those of small to midsize, have failed to respond.

A similar phenomenon occurred when the Boomer generation entered adulthood in substantial numbers and churches oriented primarily toward the Pre-Boomer generation and their families failed to adapt their ministries to accommodate the Boomer culture, its attitudes and special needs. Consequently, new churches were launched that recognized and responded to this void, and some of the prominent megachurches of today were spawned under a Boomer-oriented approach to ministries. Two often cited examples are Willow Creek Community Church of South Barrington, Illinois, and Saddleback Community Church of Lake Forest, California. Saddleback had its beginning in 1980 and has since grown to an attendance of about fifteen thousand. Willow Creek was launched in 1975 and currently ministers to some twenty thousand. Both initially directed their ministries toward the unchurched, mostly Boomers, who displayed no interest in the traditional churches of that day, which were oriented primarily toward earlier generations. The same phenomenon is being repeated today throughout America and other countries with respect to Generation X churches.

Churches today fall into one of two major categories — those that are generation driven and those that are not. We classify as generation driven the rapidly growing number of Generation X churches, the Baby Boomer churches, and the relatively few large generation based multicultural churches that have ministries designed to meet the needs of all generational categories. The largest body of churches, most of which are small to midsize in terms of attendance and emphasize a one-size-fits-all ministry approach, can be classified as not generation driven. In ensuing discussion we refer to this second category as "Caretaker churches" since they are primarily oriented toward churched believers and their families. Attendance at Caretaker churches may include a broad age range, but generally they are families or individuals who have a church background and feel comfortable in a ministries setting that has carried over for many years, as opposed to the contemporary format and other distinctives that characterize churches oriented primarily toward reaching the unchurched Boomer and X generations. The subject is introduced at this point to identify the major thrust of this book. The large number of established churches in America that fall under the "Caretaker" classification face an uncertain future. A vast market of mostly younger unchurched Americans represents the primary evangelistic challenge of our day, and Caretaker churches are not structured to reach it. Unchurched Generation Xers and, to a lesser extent, Boomers have been indoctrinated into a postmodern mind-set, have largely rejected conventional churchianity, and are most effectively reached using new methods and approaches.

Figure 1-3 provides an overview of church types, their current ministry orientation, and the realistic options open to them. Caretaker churches have the option of continuing on their current course of little or no evangelism and conversion growth or launching a new outreach to either unchurched Boomers or Generation Xers. Boomer churches can either remain oriented toward a Boomer ministry or expand their outreach focus to include Generation X. The most logical course for Generation X churches is to continue what they are doing — remaining singularly focused toward Generation X. Relatively few churches are geared to reaching this strategically important generation, which requires a different type of ministry. Similarly, "continue the same" is the indicated course for multigenerational churches, based on the premise that they already have ministries designed to meet the unique requirements of each generational category. The primary focus of this book is on Caretaker churches and their revitalization through the options indicated that involve a generation driven reorientation leading to conversion growth.

For Caretaker churches that consider evangelism to be a primary purpose, a generation driven approach to ministries represents an imperative, rather than an option. From data indicating the lack of church growth in America, it is evident that very little evangelism is taking place in Caretaker churches, the reason being that the ministries of these churches are designed primarily to accommodate believers, rather than the unchurched. Changing this orientation represents a major challenge for small to midsize churches, partly due to resource constraints, but mostly because of the need to adapt to differing ministry agendas for established churchgoers versus unchurched Boomer and younger generations.

Figure 1-3

BASIC OPTIONS BY CHURCH TYPE

Church Type		Current Ministry Orientation	Realistic Options
Not Generation Driven	Caretaker Churches	• Churchgoers	Continue the same
		• Some unchurched youth & children	Expand outreach to unchurched Boomers
		• No significant outreach to unchurched adults	Expand outreach to unchurched Generation Xers
Generation Driven	Boomer Churches	• Churched Boomers	Continue the same
		• Unchurched Boomers	Expand outreach to unchurched Generation Xers
		• Some unchurched youth & children	
	Generation X Churches	• Churched Xers	Continue the same
		• Unchurched Xers	
		• Some unchurched youth & children	
	Multi-Generational Churches	• Churchgoers	Continue the same
		• Unchurched Boomers	
		• Unchurched Xers	
		• Unchurched youth & children	

Generation driven churches, on the other hand, experience high levels of conversion growth, reflecting success in evangelism for the very reason that Caretaker churches are not. Their ministries are designed to respond to the cultural needs, attitudes, and thought processes of the unchurched in the generational categories they have targeted.

Optimistically, many Caretaker churches do have the option to adapt and make changes to their ministries approach that will make them more relevant during this era of change and beyond. And it should be possible to do so without compromising basic core values or their commitment to long-established congregations that are oriented toward traditional ministry formats that have prevailed over the years.

The challenge of change

The option open to Caretaker churches translates into the challenge of change. Unfortunately, one of our strongest human characteristics is resistance to change. Historically, most established organizations have found it extremely difficult to intentionally introduce new products, programs, or services that will displace those that are well entrenched and have been at the heart of past success. That's why Boeing displaced Douglas as the world's leading commercial aircraft producer after it introduced the first viable jet-propelled commercial transport aircraft, while Douglas chose the lower-risk option of staying with propeller-driven models until it was too late to catch up. That's also why Douglas no longer exists. After merging with the McDonnell Aircraft Company in an attempt to survive, Douglas was subsequently taken over by Boeing.

A more recent example in the corporate world is Montgomery Ward & Co., the retail chain founded in 1872 that helped pioneer American retailing through mail-order catalogs. Sears Roebuck & Co., its major competitor in the early years, was not founded until 1886 and did not put out its first general-merchandise catalog until a decade after that. And yet Sears moved rapidly past Montgomery Ward after World War II with an aggressive expansion of retail stores, while the pioneer continued to emphasize the mail-order side of its business. By the time Montgomery Ward changed its policies to reflect changing American life, it was too late, and after years of trying to catch up, the chain declared bankruptcy in December 2000. Other more innovative chains, including Home Depot, Best Buy, and Target, as well as its old nemesis, Sears, simply passed the pioneer merchandising company by. Innovative marketing had launched it into pre-eminence, and resistance to change and the absence of innovation led to its ultimate demise.

Churches face the same basic problem — coping with change. In a similar fashion churches can become so committed to past programs and worship formats that they become ends in themselves, rather than means to an end. This argues for churches to have a well-defined mission statement, usually expressed in terms of specific purposes, and to view programs and ministries as the means of implementing such purposes. In a sense, programs are a format for marketing and promulgating spiritual ideas or concepts. As the market or culture changes, churches must maintain flexibility to change or adapt marketing methods as appropriate in order to remain relevant and effective in fulfilling basic purposes. (The subject of purposes in this context is discussed further in chapter 9.)

The idea of targeting specific generational categories is a change in the way churches have traditionally approached ministries. Similarly, designing programs to meet the unique needs of specific generational groups may involve significant programming changes. So, in a very real sense the major hurdle confronting church leadership in addressing how to adapt most effectively to today's generation based multiculturalism is to overcome resistance to change. This hurdle helps to explain why it is more difficult for established churches to reorient ministry agendas or approaches to a changing culture than for start-up churches, which are not burdened with yesterday's ministries baggage and inertia. Change is always risky, often painful, and is not accomplished by apathetic leaders. It requires vision and high motivation to break through the rigidities of an aging organization. But failure to institute appropriate change is to court even greater risk. Churches that continue to be guided by outdated ministry agendas with respect to younger generations embrace a sure formula for future irrelevance. But the flip side is that the conditions requiring change also breed unprecedented opportunities. These are scoped below, along with the challenge that accompanies them.

Opportunities and challenge

According to recent surveys, about 60 percent of American adults do not attend church on a consistent basis.[5] We currently have an adult population in the United States of about 200 million, which means a potential market of about 120 million adults who are not being reached by the church. The great majority of these are Boomers and Generation Xers, since they compose about two-thirds of the adult population. America is now commonly referred to as the world's third or fourth largest mission field. The fact that about 60 percent of America is unchurched raises the question as to whether these are unreceptive atheists or the church is simply failing in its mission.

A Gallup survey found that 96 percent of Americans say they believe in God, 71 percent profess belief in an afterlife, and 90 percent say they pray.[6] A Barna survey provided similar responses from adults.[7] Eighty-seven percent stated their religious faith was important to them; 74 percent wanted a close relationship with God; two-thirds claimed to have a personal faith in Christ; 39 percent described themselves as "born again," 18 percent as "evangelized," and 29 percent as "fundamental"; and 85 percent considered themselves to be Christians. So, there appears to be a spiritual hunger or yearning among almost 90 percent of Americans, but only about 40 percent are finding their way into churches. That translates into about 100 million of America's 120 million unchurched adults who say that religion is very important to them but they don't attend church consistently.

The unavoidable conclusion is that churches have a tremendous challenge and many opportunities to meet the spiritual needs of a large segment of the American adult population — in fact, a majority of them. But what lies before today's church cannot be approached as business as usual. Addressing this challenge begins with a clear understanding of the underlying changes influencing the way people think in terms of truth and reality. The key issue in this regard is the shift to postmodernism and its basic tenets, the subject of the next chapter.

Chapter two

THE RISE OF POSTMODERNISM

SINCE THE TIME OF CHRIST, several cultural paradigms or eras have emerged concerning how we view life and religion, truth and reality, and how we think (epistemology). Most authorities group them into three major eras: premodernism (30–1500), modernism (1500–1960), and postmodernism (1960 and beyond). Before we address the particulars of each, a broad overview perspective is helpful concerning the three eras and what led to postmodernism, the cultural orientation of today's society.

Figure 2-1, labeled "Truth and Reality March," depicts these three cultural eras in terms of three symbolic marchers. The first is premodernism. The character symbolizing this era carries the banner of divine revelation and authoritative tradition, which were generally the bases for truth and reality under this God-centered period. Premodernism lasted for almost fifteen hundred years, by far the longest cultural era in history, but began to falter when several discoveries and scientific findings began to nullify the veracity of much of what had been considered to be true under the authoritative pronouncements of premodernism. Conflict arose between many of the long-held views of the church and findings advanced by a growing movement of scientific discovery, human reason, and the expansion in knowledge, with this movement exerting ever increasing influence. Accordingly, at about 1500, premodernism exits and modernism, symbolized by the middle character, enters. During the modern era God was dethroned, or at least marginalized, and human knowledge took center stage. Human reason, scientific discovery, and technology were now regarded as the keys to discovering and applying the natural laws in operation that controlled the universe. People believed that over time these would provide solutions to humankind's most complex problems, leading ultimately to a utopian society. This cultural paradigm extended from about 1500 to the mid-1900s, when its foundations began to crack. Instead of the paradigm's leading to the promised land of a better world, humankind's problems and world conditions seemed to worsen and become more complex. The coup d'état to premodernism was administered by

Figure 2-1

TRUTH AND REALITY MARCH

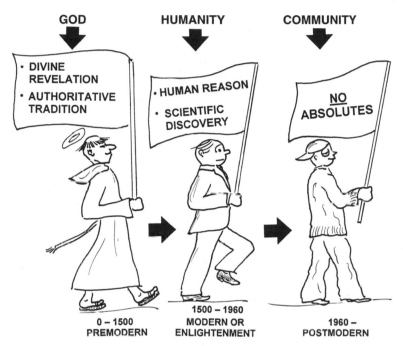

the Baby Boom generation as Boomers came of age in the 1960s. A flurry of negative events worldwide, coupled with influences and social movements that challenged the standards and cultural attitudes of the day, led to disillusionment by the Baby Boomers and rejection of the time-honored values of their forebears. The sixties revolution in moral values took shape as many of this generation rejected the basic tenets of modernism and ushered in the new cultural paradigm referred to as postmodernism.

The third symbolic marcher in figure 2-1 represents this new era. Note that human knowledge has been replaced by community as the central influence and the banner carried conveys the basic theme of "No Absolutes." All truth under this cultural paradigm is subjective and relative to situations and circumstances. What is true is what the community determines to be right for the particular group involved or affected. What is

Figure 2-2

THE BIRTH OF POSTMODERNISM
(CONCEPTUAL PHASING)

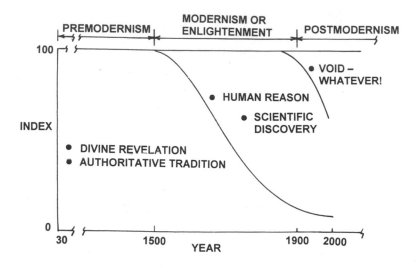

true, good, or right for one community may not be for another. Post-modernism has been characterized as an age of feelings in which there is no more truth or falsehood, no stereotype or innovation, no good or bad, but only an infinite array of pleasures, all different and all equal.

Figure 2-2 helps to explain why postmodernism was an understandable outcome after the demise of premodernism and modernism. As premodernism fell from favor, modernist philosophy moved in to take its place under a gradual transition. Marginalized and ultimately deemed irrelevant, God was replaced by a new external basis for determining universal truth — knowledge, human reason, and scientific discovery. And technology was the vehicle for applying this basis to create a better world. But when modernism failed to deliver on its promises and was subsequently rejected, the absence of an external replacement created a void. With God, authoritative tradition, knowledge, human reason, scientific discovery, and technology now all ruled out as acceptable sources for determining universal truth and ushering in nirvanic bliss, what was left? The answer is nothing.

Postmodernism represents an unfilled void that has no valid answer for determining truth and reality, right or wrong, good or bad, moral or immoral, or for providing either a rational or moral basis for the establishment of societal rules. Accordingly, "anything goes" and "to each their own" have become the slogans that characterize today's cultural paradigm. From a Christian perspective, postmodernism might at first be viewed negatively as a loose cannon in terms of spiritual direction. From a more positive Christian perspective, however, it represents a void to be filled and, as such, an evangelistic opportunity. The balance of this chapter fills in some of the particulars concerning these three cultural paradigms in the context of this overview perspective.

Premodernism (30–1500)

Characterized by people's faith in God, the premodern period held a God-centered worldview. People recognized that there was much that they did not and could not know but accepted by faith, divine revelation, and related authoritative tradition. Anselm, archbishop of Canterbury and a scholastic theologian and philosopher (1033–1109), put it in these terms: "I believe in order that I may understand." God was viewed as the source of objective, absolute truth and as the author of a divine story of which humankind was an important part. Many in the Western world defined truth in terms of Judeo-Christian beliefs and ethics based upon divine revelation provided by the Bible, tradition, or other sources. Other religions had their own sources of divine revelation. For example, Islam, the religion of Muslims, considered truth to be set forth in the Koran and the teachings of Muhammad, the prophet of their god, Allah. Other authoritative traditions looked to the era's authorities and intelligentsia for determination of truth and reality concerning matters not encompassed by divine revelation or concerning its interpretation and amplification as to standards for human relationships, moral values, and societal rules.

A number of events that began to challenge this belief system that relied heavily upon civil and religious authorities for the interpretation of divine revelation and other truth precipitated the decline of premodernism. These events include the discovery of the New World by Columbus (1492), which changed perceptions concerning the earth's geography; the new understanding, initially advanced by Copernicus, that the earth and other planets revolve around the sun, which nullified the misconception as to the earth's centrality in the solar system; the Reformation precipitated by Martin Luther, which changed prevailing concepts concerning spiritual truth; and the introduction of the Gutenberg press, which revolutionized communication and the dissemination of information. As scientific knowledge progressed, it often conflicted with church dogma, resulting in confrontation and polarization toward one or the other of two philosophical viewpoints — premodernism versus modernism — with modernism ultimately prevailing. The reception of the Copernican theory of the solar system helps illustrate this point.

Recognized as the founder of modern astronomy, Nicolaus Copernicus (1473–1543) produced a work in 1530 in which he asserted that the earth rotates on its axis once daily and travels around the sun once each year. This theory represented a radical departure from the conventional wisdom of the day. The accepted view of the universe was that of a closed space bounded by a spherical envelope, beyond which there was nothing. The earth was believed to be a fixed, inert, unmovable mass located at the center of the universe (the Ptolemiac theory). All of the celestial bodies, including the sun, were thought to revolve around the earth. The politically powerful church firmly subscribed to this view in which humankind and the earth occupied a special God-ordained centrality in the solar system. Although the Copernican theory was at odds with church doctrine, it did not become a major point of contention during the lifetime of Copernicus, largely due to his reluctance to advance his theory aggressively. Described as a perfectionist, he never thought his work to be ready or complete, pending further observation and verification. Remarkably, he made his celestial observations and developed his theory without the benefit of telescopes, which had not yet been invented. Copernicus died in 1543, never anticipating the stir his work would one day precipitate.

Two Italian scientists, Galileo Galilei (1564–1642) and Giordano Bruno (1548–1600), embraced the Copernican theory and precipitated a major confrontation with the church. Galileo, a renowned astronomer, mathematician, and physicist, encountered serious opposition from the church for subscribing to the Copernican theory and for his related teaching on the motion of the earth. Galileo, incidentally, had developed a telescope and invented a number of other scientific instruments that made much more accurate celestial observations possible than Copernicus was able to achieve. He was admonished by the church not to teach or endorse Copernican astronomy because it went against church doctrine. His failure to comply resulted in his being summoned by the Holy Office to Rome in 1632. A tribunal there passed sentence condemning Galileo and compelling him, under the threat of torture and death, to repudiate and recant his embracement of the Copernican theory and related teaching. Although he complied, he spent most of his remaining years in exile. Bruno had the audacity to suggest that space was boundless and that the sun and its planets were but one of any number of similar solar systems. He was tried before the Inquisition, condemned, and burned at the stake.

The churches's reaction to Copernicus's theory typifies the conflict and confrontation that occurred between emerging science and the authoritarian dogmatism of premodern religious institutions. Such events helped pave the way for a new cultural era that became known as modernism.

Modernism (1500–1960)

While the premodern era was God centered, the modern era became human knowledge centered. In contrast to premodernism, modernism viewed humankind as the author of its own story and marginalized God or considered God irrelevant. The keys to power and the source for determining universal truth and reality were knowledge, human reason, and scientific discovery. The modern period encompassed the Renaissance (1400–1600), the Reformation (1500–1700), and the Enlightenment (1600–1800). The latter, also known as the Age of Reason, elevated humanity to center stage as autonomous, rational, thinking beings in a mechanistic universe. Only that which could be scientifically proved or empirically justified became the basis for determining universal truth. Human reason and scientific discovery progressively replaced God in the public arena as the era unfolded.

While knowledge and science were increasingly exalted, certain absolute truths continued to be validated under the empirical method and human reason, even though they did not lend themselves to scientific validation. For example, humankind in general still recognized such values as honesty, integrity, and human dignity as universal truths, good for all people. Modernists could even be evangelized by the use of logic as a strategy to establish the validity of Christianity. For example, Josh McDowell used historical evidences as the basis for proving the veracity of the Bible and conducting an effective evangelistic ministry on college campuses and elsewhere using this approach. Although modernist thought marginalized God, it did not require atheism as the sole religious perspective but tolerated agnosticism and the belief in an impersonal God. However, modernism did not consider God relevant in the affairs of humankind or in the determination of universal truth. For example, the concept of divine creation was not an acceptable alternative to evolution.

Some of the most notable leaders during the early stages of modernism were René Descartes, Isaac Newton, and Francis Bacon. Descartes is known for the principle of doubt through human reason that placed great importance on the concept of knowing objectively. His maxim "I think, therefore I am" conveyed the idea of a new method of thought based on observable, logical, rational phenomena. His approach involved inductive rationalism and the concept that nothing was true until grounds were established for believing it to be true. Newton is best known for his work in physics and advancing the concept of a universe that functions under certain laws that can become known and understood, and thereby utilized to humankind's advantage. Bacon focused on the quest to establish control and power over nature through discovering nature's secrets and manipulating and mastering the natural world through technology. Modernism can be summed up as the embodiment of an abiding faith in the power of human reason and science to answer life's issues and lead to the creation of an ideal human society and environment.

Winds of change

However, in time reality began to set in, and the brave-new-world expectations of modernity became increasingly suspect. The "winds of change" depicted in figure 2-3 gave growing evidence that modernism was not leading to the figurative Mt. Utopia, as promised. These destabilizing "winds," or events, extend back several decades and include two world wars "to end all wars," with the Great Depression in between. The devastating destruction of life and the suppression of human rights

Figure 2-3

THE WINDS OF CHANGE

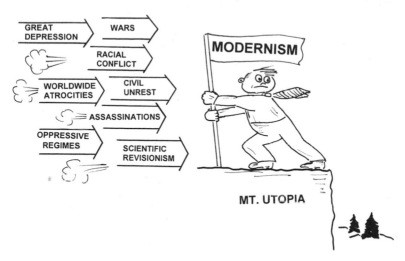

under the regimes of Joseph Stalin (Russia) and Adolf Hitler (Germany) provided further contradiction to modernist expectations of sustained human progress. Jimmy Long, in *Generating Hope: A Strategy for Reaching the Postmodern Generation*, points out that even in the scientific realm Einstein's theories advanced the view that there was no universal cause and effect principle and that scientific method could no longer be relied upon as the absolute determinant of truth versus falsehood.[1]

While the modernist system of thought had thus begun to unravel, it later fell into much more serious disrepute in the minds of the Baby Boom generation, which appears to have ultimately administered the coup d'état to modernism (fig. 2-4). Entering the scene after World War II, Boomers were born from 1945 through 1964. They are called Boomers because the birthrate for this generation surged to an all-time high. This birthrate bubble, which lasted for almost two decades, is generally attributed to several factors, the most significant being soldiers returning home after World War II, marriages that were deferred because of the war, and an expanding economy during the postwar era.

Figure 2-4

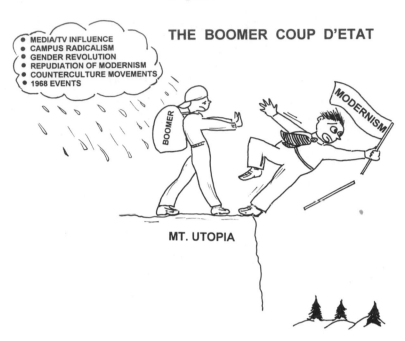

THE BOOMER COUP D'ETAT

- MEDIA/TV INFLUENCE
- CAMPUS RADICALISM
- GENDER REVOLUTION
- REPUDIATION OF MODERNISM
- COUNTERCULTURE MOVEMENTS
- 1968 EVENTS

MODERNISM

MT. UTOPIA

The Boomers came of age in the sixties. Initially, modernist philoso-phy prevailed and appeared to get a boost by early events of this period under the leadership of men like John F. Kennedy, Martin Luther King Jr., and others who sought to achieve significant human progress in several fields. These included the Civil Rights movement, landing a man on the moon, the Great Society program, which sought to eliminate poverty, and America's commitment to democracy worldwide, as evidenced by our intervention in Vietnam. The "God-is-dead" movement during this era also reflected the modernist mind-set concerning the preeminence of humankind. However, a series of upheavals subsequently brought dis-illusionment and, together with other factors that converged as Baby Boomers came of age, brought about major cultural shifts that gave signif-icant impetus to the postmodern era. Wade Clark Roof, in *A Generation of Seekers,* identifies these factors as upheaval, affluence, the gender revo-lution, higher education, and the media.[2] The Boomer generation is often discussed in terms of two waves, the first consisting of those born between 1945 and 1954 and the second between 1955 and 1964. The first wave experienced more upheavals and a better economic environment than the second, but both waves embraced the so-called new morality and change in cultural values that came into being with this generation. They also shared in an optimism to bring about changes that subsequently changed to disillusionment through a series of significant upheavals.

Political upheavals

Among the most significant upheavals in the sixties were the assassinations of President John F. Kennedy (1963), Robert F. Kennedy (1968), and Martin Luther King Jr. (1968); the Vietnam War, which began with U.S. involvement in 1963 and continued to escalate until the cease-fire (1973); the Civil Rights movement and the marches beginning in 1965; the antiwar movement that began with protest marches in 1965; and the violent confrontations at the Democratic Convention in Chicago (1968). Later came the energy crisis, Watergate, and the Three Mile Island nuclear incident. These and other events brought disillusionment to the Boomer generation concerning the institutions of society and the prevailing modernist concepts that their parents and grandparents had long held in high esteem and confidence.

By 1968, a significant movement aimed at cultural and political change was underway by radical students. Stanford's radical student cheer, "Hey, hey, ho, ho, Western civilization has got to go" characterized the attitude. These radical students rejected the traditional values of earlier generations, initiated the "new morality" and sexual freedom, opposed the Vietnam War, and basically sought to remake society in terms of cultural values. The Vietnam War was probably the most important factor in the disillusionment and loss of confidence by Boomers concerning the institutions of society and modernist philosophy. In 1965, a march around the Washington Monument attracted twenty thousand opponents. In 1967, more than fifty thousand protestors crowded onto the Pentagon steps. Many young men refused to serve, believing the Vietnam War to be unjust and unwinnable, and thousands fled to Canada or went to jail to avoid military service. While Boomers did not universally oppose the war, even those who supported it also became disenchanted in time with the nation's leadership and political institutions as U.S. losses mounted and "body counts" were reported daily with, seemingly, no end in sight.

Affluence

Boomer affluence was another important factor in the Boomer-led cultural revolution. The first wave of Boomers were born at a time that afforded opportunities their parents did not enjoy. And their indulgent parents went out of their way to lavish on their children all the opportunities and benefits that they were denied in growing up. The 1950s and 1960s were times of economic growth and prosperity. More and more Americans enjoyed home ownership than ever before, and the American dream was alive and well. The Boomers became a target of mass consumer marketing in this era of an increasingly consumer-oriented society. Middle-class Boomers soon acquired a sense of entitlement, in part due to the aggressive marketing of products aimed at this growing market segment. This affluence provided the luxury of leisure time and expanded opportunities for Boomers to challenge the values of society that existed at that time, along with its institutions, as well as to explore and define their own values. As Boomers became teenagers, many went on to college instead of joining the workforce, providing additional years and influence to invent their own culture and defer the requirement to earn a living along with the other responsibilities of adulthood assumed at that age by earlier generations.

Musical influence

A commonly held view is that much of what influenced the youthful Boomers came from rock bands and singers with their ongoing musical message, which was counter to traditional values and morality in almost every respect. Craig Kennet Miller discusses this in his book *Baby Boomer Spirituality*.[3] The ongoing drumbeat of rock and roll focused on the precarious state of life in the nuclear age, antiwar themes, the put-down of discipline, achievement, and academics, and emphasized themes of hopelessness, unfulfilled desires, and escape to a transcendent state of peace and love. With the invention of the portable transistor radio, this music became a universal language among Boomers and a significant influence in forming their values. Many experimented with drugs, which came into wide usage by this generation.

Economic factors

While the older Boomers (first wave) fared well in this era of prosperity, the younger Boomers (second wave) did not do as well. As Boomers entered adulthood in the 1970s, the economic dream of affordable home ownership and real income that allowed one working parent to support a family comfortably were still intact. By the late 1980s and 1990s, however, many Boomers found home ownership beyond their reach and both working parents to be the norm. Inflation brought high interest rates, and the problem was exacerbated by high divorce rates. Although the first wave of Boomers enjoyed substantial economic advantages compared to the second wave, the cultural changes that grew out of the experiences of the first wave carried over to the second. The greater affluence of the first wave facilitated their involvement in demonstrations, rallies, and other forms of involvement in social and political protest. The second wave lacked this advantage, which may have been a factor in the decline of political activism during the 1970s, along with the realization that radical change in the major institutions of society and its values was not going to happen. Their focus then shifted to self-oriented achievement and materialism. But while the focus and outlook of the second wave may have differed from that of the first, the drugs, music, and new morality continued, providing a cultural continuity between the two.

Education influence

Education and the media were also important factors in the cultural changes brought about by the Boomer generation. Boomers went to college at twice the rate of their parents and three times that of their grandparents, according to surveys by Roof.[4] His findings indicate that over 60 percent attended college, 38 percent earned college degrees, and 7 percent earned postgraduate degrees. Craig Kennet Miller, in *Baby Boomer Spirituality*, reports that 85 percent finished high school, 50 percent attended and 25 percent graduated from college, and 7 percent attended graduate school.[5] He compares this to 50 percent high school graduates and 10 percent college graduates for their parents' generation. Although the statistics vary somewhat, it is clear that Boomers moved dramatically upward on the education ladder. Schools exposed students to a broad spectrum of ideas and influences during the 1960s and 1970s, as they do today. At the same time that Boomers were being exposed to new ideas, the counterculture was flourishing on college campuses and encouraged students to be more open and experimental in ideas, ranging from family and sexual styles to religious views. Television also influenced values and Boomer perceptions of reality and largely displaced the influence of religious leaders, the family, literature, and other factors in terms of social values and attitudes.

The gender revolution

In terms of the sixties cultural revolution, the gender revolution had a major long-term impact. Changing rules concerning sexual relationships radically redefined patterns affecting marriage, the family, parenting, and careers. The women's movement was a significant influence in this regard in the Sixties. Women were encouraged to break away from their traditional domestic roles and return to school and pursue careers. Medical technology through the birth control pill, introduced in 1960, gave added impetus to the women's movement by helping to enable women to pursue careers with reduced concern of unexpected pregnancies. Other changes brought about by the gender revolution have been even more dramatic. Accompanying the sexual revolution that developed, cohabitation has become an accepted norm, divorce rates have skyrocketed, single parent and blended families now constitute a large part of our population, and the family is being redefined in many places to include same-sex relationships. In addition, the roles of husbands and wives are undergoing scrutiny, if not change, in terms of traditional responsibilities with respect to child raising, homemaking, and working.

Religious influence

While the seeds of postmodernism were sown early in the preceding century, the Baby Boomers cultivated it in the second half. It continues to develop rapidly under Generation X and may be expected to blossom into

full maturity under the generations that follow. Trends in church attendance support this premise. Surveys indicate that most Boomers attended
religious services regularly as children, and yet about two-thirds dropped
out of church or other religious institutions of worship by early adulthood,
with only about one-third of those eventually returning.[6] These studies
also reveal that Boomers whose parents did not attend religious services
on a regular basis were more likely to drop out. If we accept the premise
that biblically oriented religious convictions and postmodern values are
largely incompatible, religious commitment by parents and the imparting
of traditional attitudes to their children would seem to be an important an-
tidote to the transmission of postmodern values to follow-on generations.
The mass exodus from religious institutions by Boomers and the fact that
most have not yet returned means that fewer Xers were raised in strong
religious households than their parents, which might help to explain why
postmodernism is even more firmly entrenched in Generation X.

Other studies suggest that no great statistical difference exists between
Boomers and Pre-Boomers on basic religious beliefs but that a big difference between them exists on issues of conscience — c.g., moral and social
issues — regardless of whether they are churched or not.[7] The implication is that the church and parents who attend church or other religious
institutions have not been a major counterinfluence to the acceptance of
postmodern values. The carryover of nontraditional social attitudes from
Boomers to Xers, rather than diminished religious exposure, may therefore be why Generation Xers more widely subscribe to the postmodernist
perspective. What represented cultural revolution for the Boomers involved simple acquiescence by the Xers to a new cultural paradigm that
was substantially accepted by younger elements of the adult population
by the time they came of age. In any case, what appears to be set in motion
is a recurring cycle of diminishing influence for each successive generation concerning the traditional social and moral values, as well as those
absolutes of modernism that Boomers retained and, instead, increasing
momentum toward postmodern philosophy.

Postmodernism (1960–)

Postmodernism now prevails as the dominant worldview. It represents a
repudiation of modernism and its premise that humankind, armed with

human reason, science, and technology, is no longer dependent upon God, religion, or faith, but has become self-sufficient, in control, and fully capable of unlocking the secrets of the universe, all to the ultimate good of humankind. As already indicated, modernism simply failed to deliver on these promises, a fact that became increasingly evident to the Boomer generation. Science even proved to be a double-edged sword, with almost every scientific advance also having the potential for evil, nuclear energy being a classic example. Further, for every question science answered, new gaps in knowledge arose. As a consequence, a new worldview emerged with unprecedented rapidity — postmodernism — centered on the view that neither reason, science, nor divine revelation provides objective, absolute truth.

Postmodernism is a school of thought that holds all truth to be subjective, rather than rational or objective. Postmodernists are relativists, and relativism is the belief that there is no absolute truth. Consequently, there are no standards for right or wrong, which depend upon the particular situation and circumstances of the community. What is good or right for one individual, group, or society may not be for another because different people and cultures perceive reality from different perspectives and therefore arrive at different interpretations. Emotions and intuition play a role in this.

Just as God was the dominant influence under premodernism and humankind's harnessing of knowledge under modernism, so community is now at the helm of postmodernism. The community plays a major role in deciding what is truth, reality, right and wrong, and establishes rules according to what is deemed best to accommodate the overall well-being of the community. This system of thought accommodates the coexistence of a plurality of religious beliefs, along with a mutual tolerance for diversity of views and cultural expressions except for those belief systems that do not accommodate relativism and postmodern philosophy as a major tenet. Since the Christian viewpoint does not subscribe to the absence of absolutes, it runs afoul of postmodernism. Any such group that does not buy in to the postmodern viewpoint becomes an enemy of the community in the view of some segments of society and at times can become subject to intolerance and potential persecution. The term "political correctness" that has emerged basically reflects the concept of community-based conformity. In this community-oriented context, prevailing thought rejects the idea of the self as an autonomous individual. Instead, individuality and individual expression are suppressed, and the individual is subordinated as a part of the community. Just as modernist philosophy required the displacement of faith-based concepts and convictions with science-based enlightenment, postmodernism seeks to displace personal moral convictions and individual initiative with group consensus and collective solutions.

A typical example of how this plays out in society is diversity or sensitivity training, which started out in governmental institutions but is now incorporated into many nongovernmental employment settings as well. Through this training, employees are required to accommodate politically correct alternative lifestyles as the social norm, regardless of personal or religious conviction. Similarly, the indoctrination of students in public schools to a postmodernist mind-set is evidenced in much of the so-called outcome-based education curriculum, which requires conformity, or at least verbal acquiescence, to politically correct social values as a condition of achieving required academic standards. Teaching techniques in many public schools increasingly subordinate individual performance to collective or group effort through team approaches, thereby suppressing individuality in order to accommodate what is deemed best for the group and the individuals that compose it. Poor performers are "carried" by the group and thus do not suffer diminished self-esteem. Moreover, outcome-based education encourages a consensus approach to problem solving and addressing moral dilemmas and emphasizes the concept of collective, as opposed to individual responsibility. While typically justified as encouraging team effort, such teaching techniques promote group conformity, stifle independent thinking and creativity, subordinate personal moral convictions to majority views, and cloud the distinction between levels of individual academic achievement and excellence. Referred to by some critics as the "dumbing down" of scholastic achievement, outcome-based education reflects postmodernist philosophy. Parents who reject what is sometimes called academic revisionism by the nation's educational hierarchy undoubtedly account for the growing charter and home-school movements, which are facing much resistance from the public-school education establishment and the postmodern dominated governmental institutions that are largely at its disposal with respect to national education policy and related funding. Figure 2-5 summarizes the contrast between modernism and postmodernism.

Figure 2-5

MODERNISM VS. POSTMODERNISM

MODERNISM	POSTMODERNISM
Objective	Subjective
Provable Truth	Plurality of Truth, No Absolutes
Scientific Discovery	Virtual Reality
Autonomous Self	Community
Individual Initiative	Collective Solutions
God Not Relevant	Impersonal Life Force, Religious Pluralism

Almost every aspect of today's culture reflects postmodern thinking. This pervasiveness is described in the excellent essay "Ministry in a Postmodern Culture," by Philip Mason, pastor of New Earth Tribe Church in New South Wales, Australia:

Postmodern ideas are reflected in a broad spectrum of cultural expression: the arts, music, theatre, language, architecture, etc. We do not have to look very far to see that these ideas have permeated contemporary society on almost every level. Consider the changes we have witnessed in the following areas in just the past two or three decades.

1. *Dress styles.* Non-conformity is the value that reflects postmodern styles in dress and appearance. Modernist dress styles were symmetrical, tidy, neat and complimentary. Postmoderns intentionally dress to shock; non-symmetrical hairstyles, dreadlocks, body piercing, abstract, non-matching clothes, etc. All of these things are a statement of the tacit rejection of the values and standards of modernity.

2. *Architecture.* Modernist architecture reflected modernist values: unity, symmetry, repetition, and geometric perfection. Consider the cathedrals, skyscrapers and towers built under the sway of modernist ideals. Modernist architecture reflected the merging of art, science and industry. Postmodern architecture intentionally critiques the orderliness of modernism. It is often abstract and non-symmetrical, even deliberately offensive. This is also an intentional statement!

3. *Music.* Postmodern music is a classic reflection of postmodern values. The music is deliberately disjunctive, discordant and challenging to the aesthetic symmetry of classical and traditional musical styles. The orderliness and beauty of chamber music has been replaced by chaos and a wall of sound that embodies the angst of a new generation.

4. *Art.* Postmodern art intentionally juxtaposes contradictory styles in its critique of conformity and uniformity. Postmodern art brings together incompatible elements, forms, styles and textures. Artistic beauty has given way to abstraction and surrealism as an expression of the intuitive and the subconscious.

5. *Spirituality.* According to postmodernism all religions and spiritual paths are equal and are valid expressions of truth and reality within their own cultural spheres. Postmodernists are not phased [*sic*] by the fact that these separate truths contradict one another. Nowadays it is more common to hear someone say, "I have found my truth and you have your truth!"

6. *Television and Video.* MTV Video is a classic vehicle for postmodern values as it creates a series of images dislocated from an objective reality. The video culture is based on fantasy instead of any kind of concrete reality. Commercials often exploit this postmodern relativism by barraging the audience with a montage of images that are designed to alter our perception of reality. Sit-coms further reinforce the values of relativism by eroding the foundations of morality and ethics.

7. *Computer Culture.* The cyber world takes us further into alternative realities. The cyber world is a fantasy world; a world of "Virtual Reality." It is an extension of the human imagination where we can rule the world or command empires or galaxies from the keyboard. Movies such as "The Matrix" and "The Thirteenth Floor" challenge the very idea of objective reality by suggesting that our very perception of reality may be controlled by computer technology. Science-fiction has truly come into its own in the cyber generation.

8. *Social Habits.* Drug use opens doors to new perceptions of reality. These perceptions are all equally valid expressions of truth in postmodern culture. Designer drugs are manufactured to promote chemically altered states of reality. Technology is employed to explore new frontiers of human consciousness, even though they are chemically engineered. The Ecstasy generation and the Cannabis Culture are doorways into new and diverse expressions of collective reality.

The net effect of all of these social activities is to disconnect us from any sense of objective reality. We choose the reality we will live in! We make our own reality! And who has the right to impose their perception of reality upon another?[8]

From a conservative Christian perspective, the reaction to postmodern philosophy is extremely negative, reflecting the view that no good can come of it. The core beliefs of postmodernism are in direct conflict with the concept of biblically based absolutes. However, there is an upside in terms of evangelistic opportunity that must not escape unnoticed. An article in the *Mars Hill Review* documenting an interview with Michael B. Regele, author of *Death of the Church,* emphasized this aspect. Following are selected excerpts of Regele's comments in this interview.

Postmodernism actually does contribute much; it is a very positive thing that we are benefitting from in terms of a new openness to the concept of God and the need for God in our lives. Postmodern thinking has broken us free of the strict straightjacket of modernism, which, in its reductionistic bent, closed all rational doors to transcendence.

All of this recognition of the edge of modernity and instrumental, cause-and-effect rationality has served to broaden the discussion. And that is occurring in part because of the recognition that the modern experiment wasn't adequate to explain it. This is one of the most positive benefits of the postmodern era.

In that kind of world, the church is just one more storyteller among many storytellers, and we have to come to terms with that. The reality is, on the positive side, religious stories are now acceptable, and you don't have to go back very many years to see when they weren't even listened to. I was just commenting with one of my colleagues here, that on each of the last two days on the front page of the *L.A. Times* there has been a faith-based story. Now you don't have to go back too many years to where you don't find any faith-based stories in the *L.A. Times*. I think that's a function of the larger shift that's occurring in our culture away from the rigidity of instrumental rationality and modernism.

The simple concept that we no longer have to be in defensive mode, is in fact, true. If it wasn't true, then why would shows like "Touched by an Angel" or "Promised Land" or "Soul Man" — these would have been unthinkable stories five years ago on prime-time TV — be so popular? You go back five years, and every time faith was mentioned, we were always characterized in weird ways. It's just not true anymore, and that's because of a postmodern shift in the culture.[9]

The outlook for postmodernism

The Boomer generation is generally recognized as the hinge generation with respect to the transition from modernism to postmodernism. They are a blend of modernism and postmodernism. Generation X (Busters) is the first generation that is totally postmodern in orientation, and Generation Y (youth) is likely to follow closely in their path. This, of course, does not apply to sincere Christian believers across all generational categories. The Christian belief system translates into a separate cultural orientation altogether, which reflects the fact that modernism and postmodernism subscribe to foundational premises that are in direct contradiction to the Christian faith in terms of biblically based absolutes and belief that God is the source of universal truth. Accordingly, our comments with respect to generation based cultural orientation refer to the non-Christian world.

Having said this, we recognize evidence of inconsistency concerning those who claim the Christian label but subscribe to behavioral patterns more compatible with a modern or postmodern viewpoint. For example, George Barna's surveys involving youth found that behaviors among Christian and non-Christian teenagers were virtually identical in areas where a difference would be expected.[10] Although more self-described Christian teenagers subscribed to belief in absolute truth and related moral and ethical behavior than non-Christian youth, the results did not reflect the degree of difference that one might expect. To illustrate, 59 percent of those claiming to be born-again felt there was no such thing as absolute truth, compared to 78 percent for those not identifying themselves as born-again. Nine out of ten teenagers who professed a born-again experience felt that determining what is right and wrong depends on the individual and situation, in effect espousing moral relativism. Many additional findings in Barna's surveys are troubling from an evangelical perspective, but these make the intended point that postmodern influence extends even into the Christian world, resulting in a clouding of what one would expect to be a clear delineation between two mutually contradictory belief systems. In effect, postmodernism may become even more pervasive than might otherwise be expected in terms of undermining the remaining bastion of counterinfluence.

Even apart from this consideration, the ever expanding influence of postmodernism appears to be irreversible. As mentioned earlier, cultural orientation in terms of modernism versus postmodernism is largely a function of generational category. The Pre-Boomers are oriented toward modernism, the Boomers are a blend of modernism and postmodernism, and both Generation X (Busters) and Generation Y (youth) are strongly postmodernist. Based on this premise, figure 2-6 illustrates the estimated postmodern versus modern cultural orientation for the U.S. population today and ten years from now. The future outlook is based upon the projected population for today's generations ten years hence and the assumption that the next youth generation (replacing the current youth generation) will be postmodern in orientation. Keep in mind that although each of the current generational categories grows ten years older in this comparison, their cultural orientation does not change. The es-

Figure 2-6

CULTURAL ORIENTATION

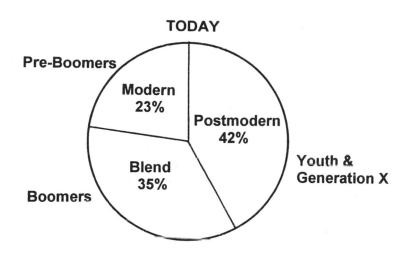

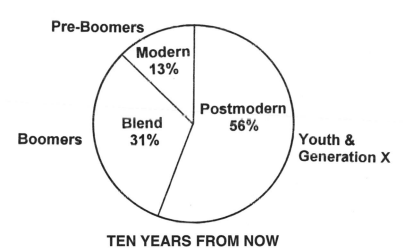

timates show that postmodernism is the major cultural influence today, and it will become increasingly so over the next decade and beyond. Representing about 77 percent of today's population, the postmodern and blended modern/postmodern cultural orientations are projected to increase to almost 87 percent in another ten years. The modernist culture drops from about 23 to 13 percent of the total as the Boomer generation gradually fades from the scene.

These estimates indicate that the cultural shift taking place is neither transitional nor a passing fad. Rather, it is a paradigm shift to a new cultural era that will dominate world society for years to come. The premodern era lasted roughly 1,500 years, and the modern era about 460 years. So, cultural shifts tend to stay with us for long periods of time. What is transitional, however, is the cultural diversity among the several generational groups, ranging from those that reject the basic tenets of postmodernism to those that embrace its cultural mandates to varying degrees. While the older population segments mostly reject postmodernism, the younger generations are dominated by its influence, and the generation of middle-agers is a blend of both. Over time cultural continuity between the generations may be expected to return, as older generations pass from the scene. But for the next decade or two the church faces the challenge of ministering to the various generational groups during this transition period when cultural continuity does not exist. What does exist are differences in cultural characteristics and spiritual attitudes that distinguish these generations from one another in important ways. This challenge is unique in the history of the church.

Chapter three

THE CARETAKER CHURCH — AN ENDANGERED SPECIES

MOST LONG-ESTABLISHED SMALL CHURCHES of fewer than two hundred average attendance, as well as some larger churches that we've defined as midsize, fall into the category of Caretaker churches. The emphasis here is on long-established, in contrast to start-up, churches. The majority of churches in America fall into this size range. Typically, a large percentage of Caretaker church attendees have a church background — most have grown up in church going families. Accordingly, a high level of intergenerational cultural continuity between the young and older adults allows a one-size-fits-all approach to ministries to work quite well.

Largely ignoring the radical cultural changes that have taken place among the unchurched Boomers and Generation Xers and how they view life issues, Caretaker churches make only limited attempts to come to terms with this reality. Their programming tends to remain much the same as it has been over past generations, with perhaps some modest changes. For example, the worship format may include more choruses in the congregational singing, the use of hymnals at times replaced by visual projection of the words on a screen, and a mix of contemporary vocal and instrumental music with traditional hymns and organ music. But for the most part, programming, leadership methods, and attitudes are a carryover from the past when the church played a somewhat different and more prominent role in American family life and in the community. The attendance typically includes a representative cross section of ages, and since most attendees have a church background extending through childhood, they often prefer the traditional ministries agenda and format to which they have become accustomed, along with the greater intimacy of smaller congregations.

We refer to these churches as Caretaker churches since they are primarily oriented toward taking care of the church family (internal market), as opposed to the unchurched or unevangelized (external market). Bill

Hull, in *Seven Steps to Transform Your Church*, provides the following insights:

> Churches older than twenty years have an annual rate of conversion that is one-third that of churches under two years of age and 10 percent less than churches ten to twenty years of age. There are at least two reasons for this. A church initially reaches out to gather enough people to support a pastor and have a church. Once this is achieved, its energy reverses from outward to inward. Church personnel are gobbled up by traditional church programs. The focus becomes institutional. The older the church gets, the more it becomes dedicated to survival for the sake of itself. This trend is creating the kind of deplorable evangelistic dearth that now characterizes more than half of our evangelical churches.... Pastors must meet the needs of the saints, feed them, be their shepherd, attend their meetings, and live up to their expectations. The focus is not on others, it is on self. The pastor becomes a chaplain. His focus is not outreach; it is servicing the saints.... The survey found the rate of retention of new people is 20 percent less in these older churches than in those two to five years of age. This is caused by those congregations maintaining they are open when in reality they are closed, and outsiders are not welcome.[1]

The Caretaker church is neither of the world nor in the world. It is basically withdrawn from the world. Caretaker churches attract few visitors, and most of the unchurched who do visit never return. They often feel uncomfortable as outsiders in a close-knit social order where the congregational focus and energies are largely inward, as Hull puts it, and they often have an entirely different perspective concerning truth in general, and religion in particular. Postmodern-oriented visitors do not accept the authority of Scripture as divinely inspired revelation from God and view Christianity as one among many religious concepts, each having something positive to offer but none having a monopoly on spiritual truth. Therefore the typical sermon is delivered on one wavelength while the listener is tuned in on another. Beyond this, they view many of the traditional attitudes of Caretaker churches as out of date and no longer reflective of the societal changes that have taken place in recent decades. These societal and attitude changes are discussed in the next several chapters, which focus on Boomers and Generation Xers, how they view life and what they expect concerning the church.

Whatever growth does occur in Caretaker churches is usually transfer growth from churchgoers moving into the community or by church hoppers. Caretaker churches experience very little real growth, which means attracting nonchurchgoers into the church and retaining them through spiritual conversion. Churches that achieve growth only by attracting other churchgoers are involved in a zero-sum game that contributes nothing in terms of adding to the body of Christ. Without real or conversion growth, the future prospects for Caretaker churches is one of decline, which is not to suggest that all Caretaker churches will suddenly disappear from the scene. Rather, it implies a consolidation process in which some churches survive at the expense of others in the survival of the fittest. In this shakeout, the Caretaker churches that survive will be those with the most to offer in terms of preaching, nursery care, children and youth programs, and facilities and those of sufficient size to maintain an adequate staff. Some Caretaker churches will survive, at least for the intermediate future, to accommodate the Pre-Boomers and the remnant of younger believers reared in the Christian tradition of their forebears. Nevertheless, in the absence of real or conversion growth along with the declining population of Pre-Boomers and the ongoing shift of younger attendees to larger churches, the decline appears inevitable.

Caretaker churches have dedicated pastors who are committed to the faith and uncompromising in a culture they see as going from bad to worse. They challenge their congregations to be faithful and diligent as personal witnesses and to invite their unsaved friends to church in order to win them to Christ. Special programs are held on such occasions as Christmas and Easter in the hope that it will attract unchurched visitors and expose them to the gospel message. Unfortunately, such well-meaning attempts at evangelism do not often produce significant results. While these efforts may attract a small number of unchurched individuals, many of whom are church drop-outs who attend church only occasionally, they fail to attract the masses of unchurched postmodern-oriented Generation Xers or Boomers. What the Caretaker church lacks in terms of effective outreach is an ongoing program agenda specifically designed to meet the external market needs.

On a more positive note, Caretaker churches have a number of things going for them that make them ideal launching platforms for new ministry outreaches targeting unchurched Boomers or Xers. They are far better equipped to do this than new start-up churches, which have been remarkably successful in such undertakings. For example, in terms of a second service oriented toward Boomers or Generation Xers, Caretaker churches already have a facility. They also have an administration structure (church board, elders, deacons, trustees, etc.) of experienced leaders in place. In addition, they have nursery facilities, a youth program, and a children's ministry to accommodate the children of these new generational outreach categories. They also have congregations of well-grounded Christians representing a broad age spectrum from which to draw in establishing the nucleus of leaders required in launching and sustaining a new outreach ministry until it can develop its own leaders. Beyond these in-place structures, personnel, and resources, Caretaker churches usually have little, if any, mortgage debt, meaning reduced monthly cash flow requirements. Their congregations typically include a significant percentage of middle-age and senior members, many of whom are disciplined tithers and givers, as well as being quite well-off financially. Since Caretaker churches are not often faced with the financial challenges of younger or start-up churches, they often have enhanced opportunities to expand the ministries agenda in a way that does reach the unchurched younger generations of today's culture.

In many ways Caretaker churches are well postured for a new type of outreach that can dramatically revitalize their ministries and make them relevant in this new cultural paradigm. Strategies for Caretaker churches in this regard are the subject of chapter 10. But not all Caretaker churches will be able to successfully make such a transition. Some will fail due to budget constraints, others due to congregational intransigence; still others because of size or location. But those that rise to the challenge of change face unlimited opportunities in outreach to a world that is waiting to receive the Christian message of hope and that is hungry for spiritual truth presented in a format to which it can relate.

Chapter four

ABOUT BOOMERS

THERE ARE ABOUT 76 million Baby Boomers in the United States. Composing 28 percent of the nation's population, they represent the largest generational group and ranged in age at the turn of the century from thirty-seven to fifty-six. Boomers are regarded as the hinge generation from modernism to postmodernism and reflect a blend of the two, for they were raised with modernist values during their formative years of growing up but adopted many postmodern viewpoints in early adulthood, at least with respect to the so-called new morality and some aspects of universal truth. Although there has been a tendency to stereotype them, Baby Boomers are not a monolith in terms of religious orientation, moral values, lifestyle, or socioeconomic characteristics. But they are a generation united in many cultural respects that set them apart from previous generations, as well as from the Generation Xers (Busters) that followed them.

Spiritual or religious orientation

In describing the present religious orientation of Boomers, two books by Wade Clark Roof provide valuable information from extensive surveys: *A Generation of Seekers: The Spiritual Journeys of the Baby Boom Generation* (1993) and *Spiritual Marketplace: Baby Boomers and the Remaking of American Religion* (1999). These books probably represent the most comprehensive data and analysis currently available on today's Boomers and how they view themselves in terms of spiritual or religious orientation. The findings are based on surveys, in-depth interviews, and field observation by Roof and his research staff dating back to 1988. A professor of religion and society at the University of California, Santa Barbara, Roof is a well-known author and commentator on religious trends in the United States. In his most recent book he classifies the Boomer generation into five subcultures: born-again Christians, mainstream believers, metaphysical believers and seekers, dogmatists, and secularists.[1]

Born-again Christians. About one-third of the Boomers surveyed by Roof place themselves in this category. Half identify with conservative Protestantism, about one-fourth with Roman Catholicism, and about one-fifth with mainstream Protestantism. In the surveys, this subculture generally refers to themselves as "evangelicals" or "Christians," and most can identify a memorable redemptive experience when the presence of Christ became real in their lives. Although this Boomer segment has diverse religious or denominational identification, they share in the experience of a "personal God" or of a "personal relationship" with Jesus Christ.

Mainstream believers. This subculture constitutes about 25 percent of Boomers. They identify with Catholic, Jewish, and Protestant religious bodies. About half of the Boomers in this category are Catholics, and over a third are Protestants who identify with old established denominations. The remainder are Jews, former fundamentalists or evangelicals, or those of other religious persuasions. In terms of beliefs, they are quick to differentiate themselves from born-again believers. Mainstream believers tend to be rooted in the religious history and traditions of the denominations or institutions with which they identify but are tolerant of other religious viewpoints, as reflected in a relatively high level of interfaith marriages. Tending to have weak ties to religious institutions, mainstream believers do not view regular attendance as a prerequisite for being a good believer.

Metaphysical believers and seekers. This group represents about 14 percent of the Boomers and is the most diverse subculture. It includes Neo-Pagans, Wiccans, goddess worshipers, Zen Buddhists, Theosophists, nature lovers, and many other splinter groups of so-called spiritual seekers. A number of Boomers in this category come from traditional religious backgrounds. More specifically, their background distribution is 6 percent Jewish, 20 percent Catholic, and 56 percent mainline Protestant. Many are dropouts from the more conventional or established religious institutions, which failed, they believe, to meet their needs.

Dogmatists. Roof lumps fundamentalists, moralists, neotraditionalists, and ritualists all together into this category that makes up 15 percent of Boomers. Many from a conservative Christian perspective would find the inclusion of fundamentalism in this category to be inappropriate. It seems to reflect Roof's view that rigidity and religious ritualism characterize fundamentalism, overshadowing any spiritual considerations concerning institutions that fly under this banner. He characterizes dogmatists as those who are religious but not spiritual — concerned more with external form than with the spiritual. Fundamentalists would be quick to point out that adherence to historic biblical orthodoxy is what the term implies, as opposed to Roof's perspective. The majority of so-called dogmatists were raised in and still identify with either Roman Catholicism or conservative Protestantism. In our view, these might more properly be regarded as an element of the born-again Christians category. Six percent are estimated to be from backgrounds involving no religious affiliation.

Secularists. Secularists compose 12 percent of the Boomer population and are likely to describe themselves as irreligious, rather than antireligious. They tend to come from mainline church backgrounds that they considered to be unduly oppressive or with which they associate bad experiences or serious doubts. Secularists are probably best characterized as agnostic or indifferent, rather than as hard core atheists.

The fact that almost three-fourths of the Boomer generation is described as either born-again Christians, mainstream believers, or dogmatists gives clear indication that they are interested in the spiritual dimension of life. Adding metaphysical believers and seekers brings it up to a little less than 90 percent. Boomer spiritual orientation or God consciousness is reaffirmed by surveys that conclude most Boomers profess a belief in God.[2] Roof's data indicates that only about 1 percent are atheists and about 3 percent are agnostics. Seventy-two percent say they definitely believe in God, and the balance either believe in a higher power or are uncertain but lean toward believing.

Other general characteristics of Boomers

Beyond religious orientation, following are other general characteristics of this generation, as summarized in *Church Wake-Up Call:*

- Low loyalty: This goes for brand name products, as well as institutions, including the church. It explains the decline of churches that have not responded to the perceived needs of Baby Boomers and the shift from denominational labels to more responsive nondenominational churches.

- Non-affiliation: Closely related, many Boomer church attendees do not become members. There is a willingness to switch churches based on need. Boomers tend to trust individuals more than institutions, making them more loyal to a specific minister than to a church or denomination.

- High expectations: Having grown up with a sense of entitlement, Boomers have high expectations from institutions. The implications are that churches that target Baby Boomers will flourish if they provide quality programs and facilities but do not require blind loyalty. This attitude of high expectations probably accounts for the high divorce and depression rates among Boomers as they experience disappointments and unmet expectations.

- Weaker relationships: Boomers are weak in building strong relationships. Related factors include high mobility and high divorce rates. Many successful churches have responded with small groups to address various needs. Examples include groups for adult children of alcoholics, athletic teams, music groups, parenting classes, employment services, cancer support, and Bible study.

- Tolerance for diversity: Boomers are very tolerant of individual differences and alternative lifestyles. This does not mean they do not have firm convictions, but are accepting of those with contrary convictions.

- Comfortable with change: Rapid and profound changes of the twentieth century have made change normal to Boomers. Churches that seek to avoid change and guarantee orthodoxy through rules and regulations find it futile. Alternatively, some older leaders refuse to relinquish control to Baby Boomers for fear they will implement unwanted changes. Such churches are destined to die with the older membership.

- Different leadership style: Whether or not Boomers have a different leadership style may be debatable. They have a tendency to be more participative, democratic, and attuned to employee needs. However, countering this tendency is the reality that leaders tend to be mentored, groomed, and molded into conformity by those over them. Regardless, Boomers perceive themselves to be different, creating a sense of generational solidarity and the tendency to push older leaders out and run things differently. Churches and religious organizations are not exempt. Unless Boomers are integrated into leadership roles, defection or institutional conflict can be expected.

- Different motivating values: Unlike their parents, Boomers are motivated more by experiencing life than by materialism. Variety, risk, and change take precedence over job security and stability.

- Seeking meaning: Boomers appear to be searchers committed to finding a meaningful philosophy of life, although they have little faith in God. Churches seeking to relate to them will need good facilities (modern nursery facilities and good programs for children).[3]

Although these are general characteristics, most have ministry implications, which are discussed in the next chapter. Doug Murren, in his book *The Baby Boomerang*, mentions several other characteristics, which are of a more church-specific nature.[4] One is that Baby Boomers are very pragmatic and are attracted to how-to sermons and a teaching emphasis that relate more directly to their lives. Boomers are also very strong in their view that women need to be involved and recognized in places of leadership and responsibility in the church. This reflects the change in attitude concerning women's roles in society ushered in by the gender revolution. Murren also emphasizes that Boomers expect the contributions of singles to be accepted to a much greater degree than they have in the past. This reflects the high proportion of singles in the Boomer generation, compared to earlier generations, and will challenge the general bias in many churches toward married individuals in terms of leadership roles and ministry emphasis.

Dropouts and the return to church

Much has been written about the high dropout rate of Boomers from church. About 60 percent dropped out during their adolescence or adulthood for a period of two years or more, although most (about 90 percent) were raised in a religious tradition.[5] The secularization of modern society rendered religious ideas and influence less relevant to the Baby Boom generation. Some left because they felt the church was unduly removed and uninvolved in addressing the ills of society.

Many Baby Boomers are now returning to the church — the so-called Baby-Boomerangs — but are generally very different from their parents in terms of spiritual outlook and biblical values. Surveys reveal that roughly one-third of the dropouts have returned to religious activities.[6] But that means the largest portion of dropouts have not returned. These remaining religious dropouts represent about 40 percent of the Baby Boomer population. Those that have returned have much less rigid views than traditionalists concerning morality, homosexuality, cohabitation, abortion, marriage, marijuana use, and similar social issues. They are also less loyal to institutions, including the church, compared to their peers who did not drop out. A high proportion of returnees may be expected to explore different religious traditions, rather than to settle into strong denominational loyalty or stay with a particular tradition.

Boomers tend to regard themselves as spiritual or spiritual seekers as opposed to religious. "Religious" connotes institutional or conformity, which Boomer dropouts rebelled against earlier in their lives. Their outlook is conducive to accepting a wide range of nontraditional beliefs. Boomers regard religion as a positive thing if it enhances their life in some way, which is much the same philosophy they apply toward most activities. They are looking for churches that meet their needs, as opposed to opportunities for service.

Researchers generally agree that the reasons Boomers are returning to church are basically twofold: (1) parents have decided their children need spiritual grounding, and (2) older adults have begun to feel their own mortality and are seeking spiritual fulfillment.[7] Some writers characterize it as spiritual restlessness. Many Boomers may say they do not believe in absolute values, but they also do not want their children to grow up without moral values. One survey found that married Baby Boomers are three times more likely to return to church if they have children.[8]

Although Boomers are exhibiting a renewed interest in spiritual matters, many do not necessarily equate this with church attendance. Boomers approach religion on a different basis than earlier generations have done. They embrace the concept of choice without commitment. Still, research on the subject generally concludes that Boomers are spiritually hungry, as evidenced by their search for spiritual fulfillment through dabbling in America's spiritual cafeteria. Figure 4-1, which is based on interpretation of the data discussed in preceding paragraphs, attempts to

Figure 4-1

BOOMERS' SPIRITUAL ORIENTATION

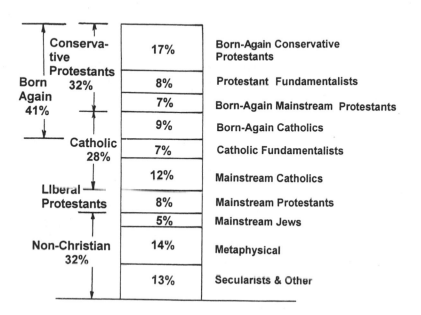

illustrate the religious orientation of Boomers, regardless of whether or not they attend religious services. While the indicated distribution is not represented as precise, it does represent a fair approximation of current Boomer spiritual orientation. The challenge facing the church today is to fulfill the spiritual hunger this seems to imply, particularly for those who are still searching.

Statistics also show that only 1 percent of the Boomers are atheists, suggesting that almost all are receptive to spiritual matters. From an evangelical Christian perspective, the fact that over 50 percent define themselves as something other than born-again believers or dogmatists (primarily evangelical Christians categorized as fundamentalists due to their strict interpretation of the Bible) must be viewed as a major outreach potential.

Chapter five

REACHING UNCHURCHED BOOMERS

A NEW TYPE OF CHURCH oriented toward Baby Boomers began to appear on the scene in the mid-1970s. Willow Creek Community Church, located near Chicago, was launched in 1975. Saddleback Community Church in Orange County, California, had its beginning somewhat later in 1986. Some established churches also began to update their ministries to accommodate the changing culture. The seventy-four-year-old Second Baptist Church of Houston, which updated its ministry approach in 1978, has since grown from a few thousand to about twenty-four thousand. Many of these Boomer-friendly churches that broke from tradition are now megachurches. Most were launched when the average age of Boomers was in the mid-twenties. New Boomer churches grew rapidly because they responded to the cultural and spiritual needs of a large young Boomer population that traditional churches of that day failed to accommodate.

Bill Hybels began Willow Creek by going door-to-door and surveying why people in the area did not attend church. His survey included such responses as the following: churches focused too much on getting money; the music was not appealing; many could not relate to the messages; the services were boring or irrelevant; churches did not meet their needs; people were made to feel guilty or ignorant.[1] Rick Warren, who founded Saddleback Community Church, also conducted a door-to-door survey during the first twelve weeks after moving to Saddleback.[2] These churches were successful because they studied the market and were responsive to the cultural and spiritual needs of those in the communities involved. Saddleback Community Church, without owning a building, grew to ten thousand attendees during the first fifteen years, during which time seven thousand people gave their lives to Christ. The church now ministers to about fifteen thousand attendees; Willow Creek ministers to about twenty thousand. Megachurch status and large modern facilities at the outset were not prerequisites to accomplish this growth.

Today's Boomer churches

But that was then. The average age of Boomers is now in the mid-forties and ranged from thirty-seven to fifty-six at the turn of the century. The Boomers have not only matured, but their situation has also changed. A large portion are now married or divorced, have children, are settled into careers, and many are well on their way to meeting self-fulfillment and financial aspirations, a primary focus of this generation. They are also struggling with life issues that they did not face as twenty-year-olds when the Boomer new church movement began. These include problems related to divorce, single parenthood, blended families, drug and alcohol abuse, teenage children, career disappointments, and others of a similar nature. Many of the churches that minister effectively to Boomers today have a much more diverse ministries agenda than the start-up Boomer churches of two or three decades ago, even though the overall cultural orientation of Boomers remains much the same. Boomer expectations are now more demanding than when they were younger.

Churches that appeal most to Boomers today are large churches with modern facilities that offer a diversity of activities and programs designed to address their wants, as well as to satisfy practical needs. They are mostly full-service or megachurches. They provide such benefits as first-class nursery facilities, day care during church events, excellent programs for children and young people, classes on topics of concern to Boomers, networks of support groups, and social services. Some even provide sports facilities and activities, aerobics classes, live theater, and evening programs for working members.

With this kind of appeal, where do the small- to medium-size churches fit in? Or is the Boomer outreach beyond the scope these days of all but full-service megachurches? We believe the answer is that small to medium size churches still have the opportunity to attract a segment of the Boomer population who are unchurched. One factor favoring smaller neighborhood churches is accessibility and convenience. In a high percentage of Boomer marriages husband and wife both work, and a church closer to home makes it much easier to get the kids to their programs during the limited nonworking time available. Secondly, there are a large number of single Boomer parents. Once again, accessibility is an important factor. In addition, the more intimate environment of a close-knit church family where everyone gets to know one another is an appealing positive feature to such single parents.

As mentioned earlier, about 60 percent of the Boomers currently attend church or other religious institutions. Many of these "loyalists," as Wade Clark Roof refers to those who did not drop out, have remained in the small- to medium-size churches. They provide a positive influence in attracting unchurched Boomers seeking spiritual fulfillment and a church in which they can find fellowship and feel comfortable.

Criteria for attracting Boomers

While these are positive factors in establishing an outreach to unchurched Boomers, they are not adequate in themselves. Attracting Boomers requires a Boomer-friendly atmosphere. In his book *The Baby Boomerang*, Doug Murren provides an in-depth treatment concerning ministry aspects important or essential for an effective outreach to unchurched Boomers.[3] Key points are summarized below:

1. *De-emphasize membership*. Churches need to emphasize participation but not membership. Boomers are nonjoiners. They attend church, not to join, but rather to experience something. Murren recommends offering participation but downplaying membership and emphasizing the individual rather than the institution. Many traditional churches limit participation to those who are members. One way Murren has found to handle this is to create a special category of nonmembers known as "participants." Participants must subscribe to the church's doctrinal beliefs, agree to provide financial support, and demonstrate volunteer involvement over a designated period of time. In effect, participants become much like members with comparable rights while avoiding the psychological barrier to long-term commitments.

2. *Don't expect blind institutional loyalty*. Boomers have low denominational loyalty. Their lives involve heavy demands and limited discretionary time since both parents typically work. Supporting their children's activities occupies much of their free time. Accordingly, a church that is conveniently located and accommodates their needs takes precedence over denominational loyalty. They dislike

the formality that the term "institutional" implies and look for stable congregations that emphasize an informal, caring environment and are heavy in terms of the personal touch. Murren calls this a "high-touch" environment in a high-tech world, emphasizing small groups that provide person-to-person interaction. They are seeking a church where the congregation is cemented together through relationships, rather than creeds or doctrinal statements. Informality in terms of service format, dress, and avoiding the use of titles is an integral part of this noninstitutional emphasis.

3. *Accommodate their desire for experience.* Boomers want to experience life rather than hear about it. They grew up in an experience-oriented age, including the sixties culture that seemed desperate for personal experience and altered states through drug experimentation. Boomers returning to church reject the sterile, antiseptic environment of many traditional churches and seek those that they feel provide a sense of God's presence in their lives. Pentecostal and charismatic groups are growing for the singular reason that their theology is friendly toward personal experiences. Noncharismatic churches need to emphasize participation through praise songs and testimonies relating to God's working in the day-to-day lives of church attendees through answered prayer and personal fulfillment.

4. *Emphasize "how-to" messages.* Boomers want to know how God is involved and relevant in their lives. They are looking for life related messages that have practical application. They don't come to church just for the sake of learning. Representative how-to topics might include how to have a happier marriage, handle money better, deal with an unhappy job situation, acquire employment, be a better parent, and manage one's time. The challenge is to address such issues from a biblical perspective and to demonstrate God's relevance in every aspect of daily life.

5. *Recognize the importance Boomers place on women in roles of leadership, authority, and responsibility.* The church has traditionally been male oriented in these areas. In today's society 80 to 90 percent of women work outside of the home. Boomers no longer regard the role of women as secondary to that of men; they view churches that do not have women in leadership roles as out of date and perhaps

bigoted. Nor is tokenism acceptable, which Boomers will recognize for what it is. Husband-and-wife leadership teams are particularly desirable since both often work today, resulting in limited time together.

6. *Accept and celebrate the contribution of singles.* About half of our population currently consists of singles, who include single mothers, single fathers, the never-marrieds, teenagers who have left home, and widows and widowers in growing numbers as our life expectancies increase with the marvels of modern medicine. And yet, the church continues to gear its ministries to married couples and families. The Boomer population has the highest percentage of singles in our history. In the past, singles beyond the youth age level were regarded as a minority, too small in number to justify special attention. This attitude continues to prevail even though society has undergone dramatic changes over the past several decades. This bias is reflected in the selection of church leaders, couples-oriented social events, communication styles that use illustrations largely related to the 1950s world of *Leave It to Beaver,* and the carryover attitude that singles represent a small group out of the congregational mainstream.

Churches that seek to reach out to Boomers need to reorient from this mind-set, recognize the large proportion of singles in today's culture, and focus upon their needs with no less commitment and imagination than have been directed toward married couples and families. This translates into representation on church boards and other leadership responsibilities, perhaps separate services for singles, and programs that are designed to meet their needs. Murren emphasizes the importance of understanding singleness as a recognized phenomenon, emphasizing its acceptance in the life of the church, encouraging and celebrating single ministers, giving special attention to the needs of single mothers and fathers, and presenting marriage in a more balanced and realistic perspective. For churches too small to start separate single services, Murren suggests networking with other groups of singles.

7. *Respond to the high level of dysfunctionality in this group.* Boomers experience problems rooted in drug abuse, alcohol, broken homes,

and sexual promiscuity. Although these problems tend to moderate as the Boomers mature, this generation's experimentation with drugs, alcohol, and sexual aberrations has ongoing consequences. The church needs to be prepared to work with and counsel venereal disease and AIDS victims; those with homosexual tendencies; those who have relapsed into pornography, alcohol, drug addiction; and those suffering from related marital, emotional, and abuse problems. Murren's church addressed the issue with the establishment of several support groups: AA (Alcoholics Anonymous), Al-Anon (a group growing out of AA for nonalcoholic friends and relatives of alcoholics), ACOA (Adult Children of Alcoholics), a group for those with eating disorders, and an Agape Group for those with sexual addictions or disorders. Smaller churches would find it difficult to establish programs to meet all of these needs, but most could launch an AA program. The other option is to network with other churches and addiction clinics in the area. This aspect of Boomer outreach also requires an educational process through sermons or messages on various addictions and the ministry of breaking these destructive patterns of addiction that have been such a factor in the lives of many Boomers.

8. *Innovate and activate.* Two other points emphasized by Murren are that Boomers applaud innovation and have a sense of destiny. They like diversity and options, such as multiple service times plus variety in terms of small-group activities. Boomers want to have an impact on society and are oriented to activism, as opposed to having a passive approach to life's issues.

Beyond these considerations Boomers expect excellence, despise mediocrity, and enjoy variety and spontaneity. Excellence in nursery facilities and in programs for children and youth is a must. Baby Boomers also want a church that is open to controversial topics, rather than one that represses discussion on viewpoints that do not rigidly conform to church traditions and beliefs. To illustrate, we have observed that controversial issues raised in tradition-oriented Caretaker church Sunday school classes are often quickly dismissed or passed over if they encroach upon or are controversial with respect to denominational party-line edict. Discussion on such matters is suppressed, and the questioner is often made to feel uncomfortable and out of sync with the church mainstream. However, since Boomers are less bound by tradition and more accustomed to making choices in every facet of life, including religion, denominational or doctrinal dogma cannot be imposed on them apart from a rational basis for acceptance.

The music issue

Another important issue that must be addressed in considering an expanded outreach to Boomers is music. Unchurched Boomers are drawn to churches where the music is contemporary. To those who have grown up in a different musical era, the music of the Baby Boomer culture can be very distasteful. Music is like a language that one grows up with. Once it becomes imprinted in our mental system, other languages are very difficult to learn. Children pick up languages quickly, while adults must struggle to learn a new language. The same is true of music. I grew up during the big band era of "swing." Glenn Miller's recordings elevated me into a state of acoustical ecstasy. One day I asked my father to come to my room to listen to my latest Glenn Miller recording — it was the classic "Tuxedo Junction," an all-time great in my generation. Even though he normally regarded anything other than classical music or old-time folk songs like "Home on the Range" as discordant noise, I thought it absolutely inconceivable for anyone not to be emotionally moved by this new Glenn Miller sound, which literally sent chills up and down my spine. He listened to the record, but the blank expression on his face was clear communication that to him it was just the same old nonsensical discordant noise.

The Boomer generation grew up with contemporary music. It's their musical language. To them, the wonderful old traditional hymns that bring tears to the eyes of older parishioners are just old songs that are boring, with lyrics that are hard to understand and without appeal or emotion. So if reaching unchurched Boomers is the goal, it's imperative to communicate in their musical language, rather than to expect them to learn that of another generation.

For an excellent discussion on music in the church, chapter 15 of Rick Warren's book *The Purpose Driven Church* is must reading.[4] Saddleback, where Warren is senior pastor, is a contemporary music megachurch. It's been referred to as the "flock that likes to rock." Warren points out that the rejection of new musical styles is not new. When "Silent Night" was introduced, a prominent church music director of that day described it as vulgar mischief void of all religious and Christian feelings. Similarly, church leaders of another day condemned Handel's *Messiah* as vulgar theater and having too much repetition and not enough message. The queen of England criticized music John Calvin had put together to express his theology, using secular songwriters of the day. The music for Martin Luther's "A Mighty Fortress Is Our God" is from one of the popular tunes of his day. Music changes from generation to generation, and the church needs to recognize this, accommodate rather than fight or resist it, and use the musical language of the generation it has targeted to reach. Warren's Saddleback Church made the decision to stop singing hymns at their seeker services and to use contemporary/rock style instead. Saddleback exploded with growth within a year following that decision, and although they lost hundreds of potential members as a result, they attracted thousands more because of it.

A decision to initiate a ministry targeting unchurched Baby Boomers involves major changes that will be extremely controversial in a Caretaker church. In addition to the music issue, the total thrust of such a ministry represents a radical departure from the traditional emphasis ingrained in Caretaker church ministry. The most practical way to launch such an outreach is through separate services. Strategies along this line are discussed in chapter 10.

Recommended reading

Anderson, Leith. *Dying for Change.* Minneapolis: Bethany House, 1990.
Finzel, Hanz. *Help! I'm a Baby Boomer.* Wheaton, Ill.: Victor Books, 1989.
Murren, Doug. *The Baby Boomerang.* Ventura, Calif.: Regal Books, 1990.
Warren, Rick. *The Purpose Driven Church: Growth without Compromising Your Message and Mission.* Grand Rapids, Mich.: Zondervan, 1995.

Chapter six

ABOUT GENERATION X
(BUSTERS, 13TH GENERATION)

GENERATION X, the offspring of the Baby Boomers, ranged in age from twenty-one to thirty-six at the turn of the century (2001). They had a growing up experience much different from their parents. As mentioned earlier, the Boomers were raised in an environment of stable families that were largely child centered, with stay-at-home moms, and during a period of relative affluence. Their indulgent parents saw to it that they received most of the good things and advantages in life. When they graduated, good jobs were plentiful. It was an era when both blue-collar workers and white-collar workers, as they were then called, were able to realize the great American dream without the necessity of both parents working in order to make ends meet.

Things were much different for the Xers, or Busters. The Boomers did not have the same values as their parents. Self-fulfillment largely displaced child rearing as their number one priority in life. Skyrocketing Boomer divorce rates and working parents resulted in a dysfunctional family environment for a large percentage of Generation Xers. They are a generation of children raised under the trauma of divorce, single parenthood, working moms, blended families, and sometimes a succession of stepparents. Close to half of all Xers are children of divorce. They were forced into unwanted relationships with stepparents and stepsiblings, and the absence of good adult role models further compromised what was once considered a normal childhood. As infants and very young children, many spent much of their lives in day-care centers. The term "latchkey kids" was introduced into the American vocabulary to describe the large numbers of kids with a house key hanging around their neck who came home from school to an empty house while both parents were still at work. The general devaluation of children during this period is reflected not only in the higher priority placed by Boomer parents on other life pursuits but also by the legalization of abortion.

The Xers were also victims of a shortchanged childhood. Instead of coming home from school and going out to play with friends, as their parents did, many of these kids from broken homes or with working parents had responsibilities and chores around the house normally reserved for adulthood. Typical examples include doing the dishes, cleaning up around the house, shopping for groceries, and taking care of younger siblings until their parents or parent got home from work. When they became teenagers, many found it necessary to take on part-time employment (particularly teens with divorced or single parents). Because their parents were often absent from the home, television often became the Busters baby-sitter, teacher, and best friend. Xers spent hours in front of TV sets while growing up, and some latchkey kids developed a survival syndrome, as Tim Celek and Dieter Zander put it.[1] Fear can build up as young children, home alone, are instructed not to answer the door, keep it locked, close the curtains, not to answer the phone except for a certain ring code, and call 911 in the event of an emergency.

When the Xers came of age and were ready to enter the workforce, they were in for further disappointment. The job opportunities that existed during the Boomer entry level years (late 1960s and early 1970s) were no longer the same. In *13th Gen: Abort, Retry, Ignore, Fail?* Neil Howe and Bill Strauss reveal that between 1973 and 1990 real median income (inflation adjusted) for family heads under age thirty dropped 16 percent. During the same period, real income increased 39 percent for family heads age sixty-five and over, and 4 percent for those age thirty to sixty-four.[2] The Xers clearly entered a much less favorable job market than their parents. Part of the reason was the higher growth rate of so-called white-collar versus blue-collar jobs.

Employment in management, technical services, and professional specialties grew rapidly and paid well. Good paying blue-collar jobs, like precision production and craft work, grew at very modest rates, while low paying service occupations experienced high growth. So, while there was good employment for professionals and those with high-tech skills, the blue-collar employment that also provided good wages and a comfortable living for those who chose not to go on to college or other specialized training was much more limited when the Xers entered the workforce. Many of those jobs were exported abroad to low labor rate countries in the trend toward internationalization. In this international industrial rebalancing, advanced industrialized countries focus on the more sophisticated high-tech industries that are generally not labor-intensive, while developing countries specialize in labor intensive manufacturing industries that emphasize manual, rather than intellectual and technical skills. Adding to this trend, the rise of new industries in today's era of information technology and the demise or downsizing of yesteryear's heavy manufacturing industries are making job stability and security much more uncertain. Increasing price competition from rapidly industrializing low labor rate countries and the large influx of legal and illegal immigrants are other factors contributing to downward pressures on wage rates for service and lower-skill employment. The end result of all this is a generation considered to be the first in many years that is not achieving a lifestyle superior to that of their parents.

Apart from the dysfunctional family experience and the changed vocational environment, the most important influence in shaping Xers into who they are is the postmodern philosophy into which they have been indoctrinated. Their Boomer parents were the first generation to embrace elements of postmodernism to a substantial degree and were a major factor in passing these values on to their children.

Beyond parental influence, the Xers grew up in a society that can only be characterized as postmodern friendly and, to some, biased. Evidence of this abounds. Public school curricula no longer include materials of a religious nature; all views of morality is included in curricula; alternative relational lifestyles are celebrated in public parades; instruction in sexual techniques and condom use is discussed in public schools, sometimes to the exclusion of abstinence curricula; the Boy Scouts of America, which voted to exclude gay scout leaders in 2001, continues to address those who disagree with their decision; legalization of same-sex marriages, the redefinition of the family, and abortion are being debated and interpreted in federal and state governments and courts; diversity training, which for some may violate religious convictions, is a mandatory requirement for employment. Under these many influences, Generation X has been conditioned into a postmodernist mindset, which has significant implications for understanding this generation and its characteristics.

General characteristics

Our earlier book, *Church Wake-Up Call,* provides a summary of the characteristics that describe Generation X:

- As children of divorce and dysfunctional families, many Xers face disruptive consequences. Studies reveal children of divorce often have little ambition and drift through life without goals and with a sense of helplessness.

- Divorce has made this generation less inclined toward early marriage. Later marriage and economic conditions cause many to return home after college until they can become self-sufficient.

- In terms of family values and marriage, Xers tend to put family and friends first and job second.

- They have adopted a survival or adaptive mentality and a simpler approach to life in an increasingly complex world. They anticipate a bleak economic future.

- In terms of trust, their survival mentality and the broken promises experienced during childhood tend to make them respond to deeds rather than words or symbols.

- Having learned to survive by avoiding conflict, they ignore or work around authority. They respond to people who live out what they preach.

- They are socially conscious but not in the same sense as the radical social movements of the sixties. They're not trying to change the world like their parents, but are inclined toward a one-on-one outreach to fill a need or community issue.

- Beyond changing societal attitudes toward sex, increased sexual activity of Xers is thought to relate to the lack of intimacy at home and a poor self-image.

- They have little trust in the political process.

- The painful environment of their youth (the latchkey kids, divorced parents, and abused children generation) has led to a high suicide rate, drinking problems, and vulnerability to stress.

- Perhaps most significantly, they yearn for community and increasingly satisfy this need through a community of friends — a new type of family in which they can place their trust.[3]

Because they share many of the same postmodernist viewpoints, there is a tendency to regard Boomers and Xers as one and the same, except for age. The Busters are sometimes perceived as young Boomers who are merely demonstrating the individualism of youth, but who will eventually come around and conform more closely to the same attitudes and values as the Boomers. This is an erroneous perception. The two generations differ significantly in terms of attitudes, values, thought processes, needs, expectations, and ways of operating. These difference are highlighted below.

Boomers	Generation Xers
Get Ahead	Get Along
Live to Work	Work to Live
Change the World	Survive the World
Innovative	Adaptive
Optimistic	Pessimistic
Idealistic	Pragmatic
Modernist/Postmodernist Blend	Postmodernist
Objective	Subjective

Relationships and community

Boomers tend to be results oriented. They pursue goals, targets, and missions with vigor and enthusiasm. Xers have a different focus. What is important are relationships and experiencing the acceptance and the mutual caring of community. This is reflected in a work ethic that has befuddled some employers. Xers are more likely to forgo opportunities to get ahead jobwise if it interferes with their sense of community. To illustrate, if the choice is to work overtime or on weekends in order to get ahead versus keeping a weekend skiing date with friends, the latter generally wins out. Unlike Boomers, Xers regard work as a means of survival, not fulfillment in itself.

In terms of root cause, the longing for relationships and community once again comes back to disintegration of the family structure. For many Xers, family has taken on a new meaning. The close community of friends has become the family they never had. This longing for family and community can also take on a form that is threatening and destructive to society. Street gangs represent such a manifestation. They consist of individuals satisfying the need for relationships and belonging to a community that is committed to caring for one another. Unfortunately, their antiestablishment focus translates into an agenda that is hostile to society and often criminal in nature.

Group consensus and conformity

Boomers are individualistic. Bill Gates and Microsoft typify the translation of Boomer individualism and drive into a major entrepreneurial success. They are creative mavericks who are willing to break from tradition and pursue independent courses of action that run contrary to conventional or mainstream wisdom. In contrast, Xers would rather operate as part of a group. As discussed earlier in chapter 2, this all relates to the postmodern philosophical shift in which community-based conformity is increasingly emphasized in the public school curricula as well as in other areas of the public arena.

The Xers' emphasis on a group approach to problem solving and life issues is a major departure from the American rugged individualism of an earlier era and seems more akin to the Japanese model. In Japan, group consensus is the norm, as demonstrated through our own personal experience in the business world during negotiations with Japanese firms on U.S.-Japan joint venture alignments. Japanese firms always use a team approach in negotiations, but authority never rests with such teams for key decisions. Any tentative agreement must be submitted to higher levels of authority for further group scrutiny and consensus before a final decision is possible. The more important the decision, the more levels of group consensus. Accordingly, Japanese decision making tends to involve a long drawn-out process and many meetings. The group approach has served Japanese industry quite well in terms of manufacturing efficiency, product quality, and adapting and exploiting technology. However, it has generally left them behind the United States and other Western industrialized powers in terms of creativity and innovation. Some see this as cause for concern and foresee a similar pattern emerging in the U.S. as

Generation X matures and gradually assumes the reins of political and industrial leadership. It may also have leadership implications for the church as Xers take over.

Cynicism, pessimism, and victimitus

Unlike Boomers, who are characterized as positive and optimistic, Xers have been described as clinically depressed and suffering from a victim complex. Older generations have sometimes used the words "whiners," "slackers," and "self-pity" to describe them. Xers believe they have been dealt a bad hand in life, and they attribute this in large measure to the Boomer generation. Kevin Ford, in *Jesus for a New Generation,* describes the Buster attitude as bitter because of being unwanted, neglected, aborted, and resented by their parents.[4] They feel victimized by the high rate of divorce of the Boomer generation and the resulting neglect and trauma imposed on them as children. They blame the Boomers for ushering in the so-called relational revolution which brought with it an epidemic of sexually transmitted diseases, delayed marriages, aborted children, poor role models, and robbed childhoods.

Busters see the Boomers as having the good fortune of coming of age during an era of prosperity, getting all the good jobs, and accumulating wealth in their obsessive focus on materialism. In contrast, the Xers were greeted with a scenario of poor employment opportunities, rapidly escalating college costs, and a pessimistic outlook concerning future financial security. Howe and Strauss make it evident that these are not just perceptions and a sour-grapes attitude but indeed have a basis in fact.[5] The widening salary gap between the Boomers and Generation X was cited earlier. Howe and Strauss also report that home ownership for household heads under age twenty-five dropped from 23 percent in 1973 to 15 percent in 1990. It dropped from 51 percent to 44 percent during the same period for those twenty-four to thirty-four years of age, while increasing percentagewise for those over age forty-five. Seniors are described as the fastest growing, best-insured, most leisured, and most affluent generation of elders in American history. And the growing costs of Social Security and other entitlement programs represent a huge future tax burden slated for the backs of younger generations. The difficult economic picture confronting Xers is reflected in the fact that about 40 percent of those who leave home return at least once, and more children under age thirty live with their parents than at any time since the Great Depression.

The financial aspects of life may have taken a turn for the better with the sustained economic growth of the 1990s, but continuing generational disparities contribute to a general attitude among Xers that is best described as cynical, skeptical, and pessimistic. They have learned not to put confidence in promises concerning the future. Having had their hopes and expectations deflated in the past, they protect against future disappointment by not trusting anything or anyone that offers firm absolute answers, a reaction that has significant implications for ministry outreach and approach. At the same time, Xers have learned to adjust and accommodate disappointment.

Todd Hahn and David Verhaagen describe these attributes in *Reckless Hope* as realistic, adaptive, resourceful, and accepting.[6] Busters have learned to cope. They are pragmatic about the future, know there are no easy answers, and have no illusions that problems relating to their circumstances will get some kind of a quick fix. Xers have learned to adapt to circumstances in a world subject to rapid and ongoing change. They're sometimes characterized as street-smart survivalists who are very resourceful in terms of adaptability, innovation, tough-mindedness, and persistence. They are willing to work hard to reach their goals, have become masters of technology, and are skilled at using others as resources and in networking ability. Busters accept others who are different from themselves and know how to get along by respecting and celebrating such differences. Although accepting all beliefs and lifestyles has pitfalls and is not a virtue, it does have positive implications from a Christian perspective in that it opens the door to have Christian views considered.

Passive anger

The Xers' negative expectations and experiences concerning their quality of life, childhood experience, and other disappointments have left them with emotional pain that may account in part for their involvement in drugs, loud music, and other behavioral manifestations that bring diversion or relief. Emotional pain can also take shape as anger, cynicism, hardness, and bitterness that surface as an arrogant or dismissive attitude in dealing with others. Ford offers the following insight:

The socially respectable Thirteener tends to carry out his or her anger in what psychologists call passive-aggressive behavior. They don't attack society directly and aggressively as the gang member does. They get back at society in ways that appear passive but that are truly expressions of anger. They express their anger by ignoring authority and breaking the rules. They express their anger by ridiculing and scorning the system and its icons through iconoclastic surrogates such as Wayne and Garth of *Wayne's World,* Bevis and Butthead, and the Brothers Grunt. And many express their hostility by extending their adolescence and delaying adulthood.[7]

The bottom line

To sum it all up: the Xers believe they've ended up with the proverbial short end of the stick. They resent the wide disparity between themselves and the Boomer generation in terms of quality of childhood, educational and job opportunities, and the future outlook in terms of financial security and achieving the great American dream. They face the prospect of a burgeoning senior population, mostly Boomers, loaded with entitlements, the tax tab for which seems destined to be dumped squarely into their laps. The Boomer and Pre-Boomer generations sometimes view this resentment as whining by a bunch of malcontents who feel a sense of unfulfilled entitlement and fail to demonstrate the grit and drive of previous generations to overcome difficult circumstances and adversity. There may be an element of truth in this. Each generation has a tendency to compare itself with that which preceded it and to have the expectation of, if not a sense of entitlement to an improved, or at least a comparable, standard of living. When that does not occur, as with the Xers, it can contribute to a sense of victimization and alienation toward the so-called establishment.

The resentment Xers feel toward the Boomers, in particular, and society, in general, is understandable. One can argue that the cycle of good and bad economic times reflects a quirk of fate that can befall any generation. And the Boomers and Pre-Boomers would have a case in expecting the Xers to "suck it up," to use their own vernacular, and carry on without what some see as self-pity. But when the combination of negatives with which the Xers have had to contend is added up, the compounding effect must be recognized as a uniquely difficult situation to which older generations should be sensitive and accommodating, particularly in any outreach effort. Had the Xers not been subjected to postmodernist indoctrination, nor to the painful childhood experience imposed upon them, they would probably have a much more positive outlook on life. We believe the damaging impact of these two factors to far outweigh the economic disappointments mentioned. This all represents a unique challenge to the church to structure an approach to ministry that will be effective in reaching this largely unchurched and hurting generation with the real message of hope that is found only in Jesus Christ.

Chapter seven

REACHING UNCHURCHED GENERATION XERS

HISTORY SEEMS ALWAYS TO REPEAT ITSELF. Just as a new type of church appeared on the scene in the 1970s to minister to Baby Boomers, the same phenomenon is being repeated today with respect to Generation Xers, or Busters. Media reports indicate that about 150 churches targeting Generation Xers had sprung up across the United States by 1998, and the movement is just in its infancy.[1] Once again, the reason is that traditional and long-established churches have generally failed to recognize that Generation X is a different culture, molded by unique life experiences that translate into the need for a different ministries approach. Generation X start-up churches are experiencing rapid growth, while mainline and many other established churches encounter either no growth or general decline. Boomer churches, many of which have now become megachurches, are not immune to making the same mistake as the traditional churches of the 1970s when the Boomer church era began: that is, failing to recognize that Xers need a different ministry approach from that which has proved effective for their generation. For example, Willow Creek Community Church, recognized as one of the very successful Boomer churches, was not particularly successful in reaching the Xers. Recognizing that their Boomer ministry approach was not working with the Busters, Willow Creek turned to Dieter Zander in 1994. Zander had founded New Song Church in California, a very successful outreach to Xers that had reached an attendance of twelve hundred by 1994 when Zander left to join Willow Creek. At Willow Creek he founded a ministry to Xers called Axis, which has its own Sunday evening services that are led by Xers for Xers. Zander left Willow Creek in 1998 to help start new ministries in California.

The point is that ministries to Xers involve a different ministry approach than that appropriate for other generations, including Boomers — even though Boomers and Xers share certain postmodern views, contemporary music interests, and other perspectives. Some key differences between Boomer and Generation X churches suggested by Eric Stanford in *Next Wave Web Magazine* include the following:

1. Boomer churches are much more highly structured and organized. Xer churches operate more by what Stanford refers to as "charismatic leading." Xers have a stronger emphasis on involvement in church activities and in the direction certain ministries take. They feel that God leads in mysterious ways through individual lives. Accordingly, church staffs are smaller and less controlling.

2. Baby Boomer churches are largely program oriented while Xers emphasize relationships. Church gatherings and events focus more on developing relationships than upon learning or other structured purposes.

3. Boomers demand "excellence." Xers emphasize what Stanford defines as "realness." To them it is more important that leaders be authentic than highly proficient. Xers don't focus on how articulate or polished the preacher is or if the small-group leader is a true biblical authority. They look for genuineness, unpretentiousness, and a willingness to admit mistakes, share struggles, and identify with them and their life situations.

4. Boomers are highly contemporary. Xer churches are oriented toward both the contemporary and the past. They respect past Christian traditions, while being comfortable with the current culture and its technological orientation.

5. Boomer churches are rationalistic, while Xer churches are more subjective, or what Stanford calls "holistic." Xer preaching emphasizes a storytelling approach and includes Bible stories and other Christian stories of our day.

6. Xers have a more cooperative attitude toward other religious persuasions. Some are even bothered by the walls between Orthodoxy, Catholicism, and Protestantism, and particularly between denominations. They see positive values in other congregations and denominations. Stanford characterizes Boomers as being more competitive in contrast to the Generation X orientation toward cooperation.[2]

A review of writings by those considered authorities on Generation Xers reveals certain recurrent themes as to what is required for an effective ministry. The ensuing paragraphs include highlights concerning worship format, communication approach, small groups, evangelism approach, and other factors. Recommended reading listed at the end of this chapter is provided for a more comprehensive study of these and additional subjects important to structuring a Generation X outreach ministry.

Worship format and style

Kevin Ford in *Jesus for a New Generation* identifies several principles and suggestions concerning worship services.[3] They should be creative and geared to Generation X tastes and interests and should create a sense of excitement and expectation. The goal is to make the service feel like a celebration, not a funeral. The active worship style typically includes contemporary music with a band and praise songs projected on a screen. The young audience dresses in informal attire; some sing and sway with the music, while others raise their hands in praise. Elements of surprise and shock are used to make worship fun, stimulating, and somewhat unpredictable. Alternative music, drama, stand-up comedy, video clips, audience participation or interaction, and computer-generated visuals are some of the techniques suggested to accomplish this. The extent to which such techniques are feasible depends upon the size and resources of the church. But whatever is done should be done with excellence or not at all. Xers are very media savvy and are used to professionalism in art forms.

Audience participation or interaction is an important element in Xer worship services. It might take the form of the speaker asking a provocative question, but instead of following this with a long dissertation, the speaker might ask the audience to break up into small groups of three or four to discuss the question for a few minutes. This not only helps people to get acquainted but also stimulates interest in what the speaker has to offer. Another example of audience interaction might involve a roving microphone and the opportunity for anyone in the audience to share a prayer request or express praise for answered prayer.

A typical Xer service might include the following sequence:

- Contemporary instrumental music while people are coming in and getting settled.

- Several minutes of chorus singing with the words projected on a screen, along with words of welcome.

- A solo or duet, preferably selected with the theme of the service in mind.

- An appropriate video or film clip, again on the theme of the service.

- A provocative question by one of the leaders, with the audience asked to form groups of three or four with those seated nearby to discuss the question for the next five minutes.

- A request for volunteers from several of the groups formed to relate the thoughts of their group. A roving microphone in the audience would pick up their comments.

- A brief skit on the subject.

- A brief message by the pastor or leader on the theme that provides important insights, principles, and application in terms of daily living.

- A closing chorus or two.

- Dismissal for a time of postservice coffee and fellowship. This might include lingering discussion by some of the small groups formed during the audience interaction, or by others, concerning the issues raised during the service.

Communicating

Tim Celek and Dieter Zander use four "R" words to describe communication requirements for Xers: real, rousing, relevant, and relational.[4] "Real" means being authentic, vulnerable, transparent, imperfect. Xers appreciate the authenticity of people who are willing to reveal their own imperfections. Trust displayed by a willingness to expose one's own vulnerability breeds trust on the part of those with whom it is shared. The hunger for realness by Xers may be a reaction to their heavy exposure to a disingenuous media.

"Rousing" relates to bringing to light hidden or concealed issues within the lives of Xers. Its application is illustrated by sermon topics used by Zander while pastor at New Song Church, one of which was "The Great Gift of Sex." This focused on the fact that God created sex for our enjoyment, contrary to the view often held that God is antisex. A follow-on sermon topic was "The Great Divide," which addressed why God wanted sex reserved for marriage. Zander points out that these topics brought people out of hiding and demonstrated the church's willingness to talk about issues very important to them and to do so in a forthright and vulnerable manner.

The third "R" word, "relevant," has to do with practical sermons that relate to the lives of Xers and the struggles for which they are seeking answers. They want to know what the Bible has to say about such issues as the environment, racism, and reconciliation. They want to hear about real-life examples of where God has helped people through difficult situations.

"Relational" refers to how Xers relate to each other. They want to avoid the relational problems experienced by their parents. In growing up they have not had the benefit of good role models for this life skill. One way Celek and Zander have found to communicate the relevance of Jesus is through premarital and dating counseling programs.

Messages should be geared to entry-level understanding of the Bible, and spiritual concepts introduced gradually. Religious jargon that Christians have become accustomed to using should be avoided.

Storytelling is one of the most important aspects of communicating to Xers. They don't argue with stories since everyone's story is worth listening to in their view of life. Xers take great comfort from Jesus of the Gospels. They identify with the fact that he initiated his public ministry in his early thirties, had no place to call home and a questionable career outlook. He ignored religious institutions built upon hierarchical authority systems, saw through and rejected their hypocrisy, and did not conform to those religious rules, regulations, and traditions of the day that had lost their relevance. He built relationships based upon the genuineness of those in search of truth and was not influenced by gender, racial, or other superficial factors. Kevin Graham Ford puts it in these words:

It should come as no surprise, then that the vehicle of a story is a powerful and effective vehicle for reaching Generation X. In fact, the story of Jesus seems custom-designed to give Xers a story to identify with — a story to pattern their lives after. Jesus' homelessness and rootlessness, his "illegitimate" birth, his persecution by the system, his premature death — all of these are dimensions of his story that penetrate to the heart of the Xer experience.[5]

Celek and Zander make the following observation:

Generations prior to Busters wanted answers and linear, logical forms of reasoning. They wanted messages that had several logical points that could be readily applied to life. Busters are looking for answers too. But they want answers couched in the context of life. That's why they like the Gospels and Old Testament more than the Epistles. The Gospels and Old Testament stories teach things about God and life through example, and Busters need examples to follow.[6]

Narrative evangelism uses the vehicle of the story and has proved to be a powerful method for communicating with and evangelizing Xers. Evangelist and author Leighton Ford is a strong advocate and believes evangelism for the postmodern era will focus largely on this approach, which will be discussed more fully later in this chapter.

Small groups

In addition to providing for collective worship, instruction, and praise, worship services and other large-group meetings (i.e., seeker services) provide entry points for unbelievers, the unchurched, and newcomers. Other entry points include athletic events, counseling sessions, support group meetings, special programs, and various other midweek activities. However, large-group meetings do not fulfill the need Xers feel to establish relationships and become a part of the church body in a way that allows them to participate more directly and individually. This is where small-group ministries come into the picture.

The need for community or relational ministries has grown in the current era. In an earlier day, family cohesiveness provided for love and relational support through its members. The church was a place for worship, education, and social interface beyond the family unit. As the family structure disintegrated through high divorce rates, many no longer had traditional families and the support they provided. No generation has been hit harder in this regard than the Xers. As a result the church — and society in general — are increasingly made up of individuals rather than families. Even family members that remain intact relationally become scattered geographically under the mobility and changing structure of today's society. Family members often no longer remain in close proximity to one another but become separated through employment, college attendance, and other factors. As a consequence, isolation and loneliness are common. Small-group ministries fill this relational void and are increasingly important. Properly structured, they provide lasting relationships, escape from loneliness, and the opportunity to share and resolve personal problems. Xers, many of whom grew up in broken homes and dysfunctional families, yearn for the close family relationships they never knew. Because small groups satisfy this need, they are probably the single most important type of program in an outreach to Generation Xers. Moreover, since Xers process truth relationally, small groups provide the vehicle for this to happen.

Small-group ministries are not new. However, most small groups in Caretaker and other traditional churches are either Bible studies or program oriented in some other way, such as athletic teams, choirs, evangelistic teams, musical groups, social-action committees, dinner fellowships, and others. Such small groups do not usually develop into the type of community sought by Xers. While community or relationship building must be at the heart of Generation X small groups, this does not imply the exclusion of other important functions, such as Bible study, prayer, worship, and outreach. In the case of Xers, establishing a small group in which close personal relationships develop provides the best structure for carrying out these other functions. In other words, the small group is a relational ministry that carries out certain functions or programs, as opposed to a program ministry that may or may not also provide for some relationship building.

Kevin Ford emphasizes that these small groups need to be highly relational and interactive, oriented to experience and feeling, as opposed to teaching and cognition, and to provide an environment in which Xers can share their pain with others. They also need to be innovative and flexible.[7] Jimmy Long identifies four important characteristics for small groups: community, nurture, worship and prayer, and outreach.[8]

Community. The core component is community. The small group is a place where people are sustained spiritually and emotionally through a relational ministry, which implies an environment where people can share their joys, fears, and vulnerabilities and in the process develop relationships with one another. Achieving community requires an open attitude, and usually a group composed of those that have some common interest. Most young couples with children meet this criterion. Or the common interest or basis might be the neighborhood in which they all live or a common activity interest. It takes time for the group to coalesce, learn to trust one another, and be willing to open up their thoughts and lives. For this to happen it's important that they become involved together outside of the scheduled meetings. Such activities might include sporting events, dining together, an outing to the beach, or a weekend retreat.

Nurture. Bible study is an essential component that sets the Christian small group apart from secular groups. Bible study for Xers, or postmodernists in general, is different from the traditional Bible studies of earlier generations. The story emphasis discussed earlier is much more effective than approaches focusing on the communication of propositional truth and theological facts. The parables and the life of Jesus will be new to many Xers who grew up apart from a church background. The historical books help to convey the faithfulness of God. Long emphasizes that Xer Bible studies need to be somewhat short (about thirty minutes in length), interactive, and free-flowing and they need to emphasize heart, not mind.

Worship and Prayer. Worship can include songs of praise and the use of musical instruments such as guitars, if talent within the group provides for this possibility. Prayers of praise and for specific needs shared within the group are important elements. The group can also join and sit together at the weekly worship services at church, providing a powerful bonding influence.

Outreach. The group needs to be open and a place where friends can be invited. Long emphasizes that groups that are not open to new life are groups destined to die. Groups that welcome new participants continue to grow. In the small-group setting, narrative evangelism is particularly relevant.

Good leadership is required for successful small-group ministries to Xers. Leaders must be a part of the small communities they lead and become vulnerable by sharing their stories and hurts. Long describes a postmodern leader as more of a mentor and less a supervisor. Leaders need to be people who can help others to handle their problems. As leaders are willing to open up, share their lives and mistakes, they earn the trust and respect of those in the group.

Evangelism

Proclamation evangelism involves a clear statement of the Christian message, followed by an invitation to respond. This was more effective with earlier generations than it is with Generation X. Those involved in Generation X ministries share a broad consensus that other approaches, such as narrative evangelism, small-group evangelism, friendship evangelism, Socratic evangelism, and process evangelism, are more effective.

Narrative evangelism. Our own stories are often the most effective way to communicate the gospel to Xers. Narrative evangelism involves telling God's story along with how it called into question the course of our life story, leading us to consider a new, Christ-centered perspective and direction. Narrative evangelism is not simply a testimony, although that is an important part. It also requires that we live our story with demonstrated authenticity, integrity and humility. This relational storytelling means communicating God's story and master plan for humankind and relating how our life story intersected with this plan and has now become a part of it. The personal testimony — both verbally and through life demonstration — relates how this plays out in daily life while we await the great promises of the future and all eternity to unfold. As Todd Hahn and David Verhaagen put it in *Reckless Hope:* "The best stories are our own. We can tell the stories of our struggles and joys as we live in complex relationship with God and those around us. We can tell our story of how we were rescued and how we fell in love with the rescuer."[9] This approach lends itself well to small groups in which those attending develop close relationships, mutual trust, and respect.

Small-Group evangelism. A successful strategy in recent times has been the Alpha course. Over a period of about twelve weeks, the Christian message is slowly presented in an environment of open discussion, questions, and answers. Each week small groups meet together for a meal, followed by a talk. They then divide into smaller groups to discuss questions raised by the talk. Other less structured approaches involve the discussion of a different topic for the Bible study portion of each small-group meeting. The topics ought to be those that are basic to understanding key elements of the Christian faith, such as sin, forgiveness, justification, and reconciliation, as well as those that relate to the practical issues of life. These might include such topics as loneliness, marriage, sex outside of marriage, etc. There are about five thousand Alpha courses in America and Canada. More information may be obtained from their Web site at *www.alphana.org.*

Friendship evangelism. This approach has received much attention in recent years and is really a form of personal evangelism, rather than evangelism carried out through some aspect of church programming. However, close personal friendships develop among those attending small-group meetings, providing the opportunity for Christians to befriend and influence non-Christian attendees. Friendship evangelism is a lifestyle that demonstrates what it is to live in a close personal relationship with Christ. This approach takes time for friendships to grow and the influence of a committed Christian life to impact non-Christian friends.

Socratic evangelism. Named after Socrates, this type of evangelism uses his method of inductive questions and answers. A discussion leader asks leading questions and then challenges answers that are not valid. If the discussion is open and the questioning and challenging are not confrontational or condescending, then such open exploration of issues through discussion can lead to truth. Generation Xers like to discuss and explore universal truth but resent imposed principles and rote learning. This process allows them to discover truth for themselves with assistance from others.

A successful use of Socratic evangelism requires that the discussion leader thoroughly understands the subject matter and walks the fine line of not being dogmatic or appearing all-knowing while at the same time not compromising biblical truth. This effective technique can augment other evangelistic approaches, but it requires someone who is well grounded in the faith and in Scripture.

Process evangelism. Not a method, process evangelism refers to the time frame over which conversion occurs. There is substantial support to the view that the Christian conversion of Xers is more often an ongoing process that takes a period of time. Kevin Ford, in his experience with InterVarsity groups on college campuses, has found that nonbelievers who become involved in such groups gradually grow in their understanding of the Christian faith. He reports that it may take months or years, but they come to a place where they are praying, studying the Bible, witnessing, and clearly following Christ. However, the point at which they crossed the line from nonbeliever to believer is not clear, and the students themselves often do not know.[10] Rick Richardson, an InterVarsity area director, makes similar observations. He points out that it takes longer for Xers to make a decision for Christ, indicating an ongoing process though which people are socialized into the faith.[11] Much of the ministry to Xers focuses on emotional healing, which may account for this longer time period.

Regardless of whether conversion occurs at a point in time, over a process, or in a way whereby the point in time is not readily discernible, it is clear that Xers respond differently from earlier generations. They do not often respond to invitations after a stirring evangelistic message. They appear to need time to absorb the message and observe the reality as it is lived out in the lives of Christians close to them.

Music

Music for Generation Xers is not substantially different from that for Boomers, except that it is probably slightly louder and more upbeat. It's contemporary, of course, and if you don't like music with a rock beat, you won't like Xer music. Music is their language, even more so than for Boomers. It reflects their feelings and tells their stories. Fortunately, there are Christian musicians and songwriters who can have a large impact on Xers.

Acceptance and involvement

Generation Xers need acceptance, and involvement is one way to provide this. They go hand in hand. Unlike Boomers, who are somewhat aloof and like to be left alone to make their own decisions as to when and where to get involved, the Xers need to be invited. Visiting a worship or seeker service may be a good entry mechanism, but if Xers are going to stay in the church they need to feel welcome and to be integrated into a more intimate small-group setting or some other type of involvement as soon as possible. Some churches have people who are on the lookout for newcomers and make it a point to greet them, provide a warm welcome, and then introduce them to others who will provide appropriate follow-up. Follow-up contact focuses on providing additional information about the church, its programs and opportunities, inviting their involvement, and providing further coordination in this regard.

Beyond initial integration into the church fellowship, other forms of involvement that churches have found meaningful to Xers include ministries to the homeless, after-school athletic programs for latchkey kids, leadership training, leadership roles in small-group ministries, and short-term missions. The latter can be particularly meaningful because of the life-changing impact it often has. Moreover, Xers love to travel, they embrace other cultures, and they have a lot of fun while being stretched and learning much about themselves.

Following is a brief summary of some general principles concerning Xer involvement suggested by A. Allan Martin of Dream Vision Ministries:

1. *Allow them to lead.* Allowing Xers to lead in their own projects, groups, or meetings to the extent individual talents and interests permit provides a sense of ownership. Advisory support should be provided as needed.

2. *Select practical projects.* Xers find fulfillment in practical projects that have local relevance and provide tangible evidence of results. Some examples are feeding the homeless, working in shelters, and conducting blood drives.

3. *Initiate projects that foster relationships.* Xers are looking for relationships with adults beyond the young adults who are their peers, although these relationships are also very important. Programs that involve empathetic older adults or social events that are more relationally than program structured can be very meaningful. Examples include one-on-one discipling or mentoring ministries, mixed-age

home fellowships, and integration into committee involvement (working together builds relationships).

4. *Begin by assessing their talents.* In determining how to plug young people into a church job, begin by determining their talents or special abilities. Apply creative placement to fill vacancies or to create useful new activities that match their interests and utilize their expertise. In view of Xer information age and media savvy, some examples are videography for classes or a desktop-published newsletter either for the church or a church group.

5. *Consider focus groups.* Begin an advisory council of young people who meet regularly to suggest new ideas, review proposed plans, and provide advice. Through such a group, Xers feel they have a meaningful stake in the overall direction of the ministry, and the church begins the process of developing potential leaders.[12]

Facilities

Elaborate modern facilities are not important to Xers. Some Xer churches meet in converted warehouses. However, a top-notch nursery facility is essential. If the nursery fails to meet their expectations concerning child care, cleanliness, safety, staffing, and related considerations, they go elsewhere.

Other facility considerations are not unlike those typical for most church operations. Some churches have launched their Gen X ministry in separate rented facilities rather than in the home church facility. Important considerations in this regard include adequate parking; adequate seating capacity (folding chairs are fine); kitchen facilities suitable for beverage and snack provisions, as well as light meal events (although the latter might instead be held at the main church facility if provisions are inadequate); a layout that accommodates a musical combo, skits, and other audiovisual applications; space for small group meetings or classes (this may require portable partitioning); adequate restroom facilities; storage area for equipment, etc. Under the separate facility approach, public school facilities are often an option but require a set-up and take-down effort each week. Alternatively, some churches launch their Gen X outreach using the church facility but with services held on Saturday evenings instead of Sunday mornings.

Recommended reading

Anderson, Leith. *A Church for the Twenty-first Century.* Minneapolis: Bethany House, 1992.

———. *Dying for Change.* Minneapolis: Bethany House, 1990.

Barna, George. *Baby Busters: The Disillusioned Generation.* Chicago: Northfield, 1992.

Benke, William, and Le Etta Benke. *Church Wake-Up Call: A Ministries Management Approach That Is Purpose Oriented and Intergenerational in Outreach.* Binghamton, N.Y.: Haworth Press, 2001.

Celek, Tim, and Dieter Zander. *Inside the Soul of a New Generation.* Grand Rapids, Mich.: Zondervan, 1996.

Ford, Kevin Graham. *Jesus for a New Generation.* Downers Grove, Ill.: InterVarsity Press, 1995.

Hahn, Todd, and David Verhaagen. *GenXers after God: Helping a Generation Pursue Jesus.* Grand Rapids, Mich.: Baker Books, 1998.

———. *Reckless Hope: Understanding and Reaching Baby Busters.* Grand Rapids, Mich.: Baker Books, 1996.

Howe, Neil, and Bill Strauss. *13th Gen: Abort, Retry, Ignore, Fail?* New York: Vintage Books, 1993.

Long, Jimmy. *Generating Hope: A Strategy for Reaching the Postmodern Generation.* Downers Grove, Ill.: InterVarsity Press, 1997.

Warren, Rick. *The Purpose Driven Church: Growth without Compromising Your Message and Mission.* Grand Rapids, Mich.: Zondervan, 1995.

Chapter eight

CHILDREN AND GENERATION Y (MILLENNIALS)

MINISTRIES TO CHILDREN AND YOUTH are an important part of any strategy by Caretaker or other churches seeking to expand their ministries to reach unchurched Boomers or Xers. In their selection of a church, both place a high priority on the quality of ministries to the younger members of their family. More important, effective ministries to children and youth are vital because they represent the generations in which lives are shaped in terms of values and from which most Christian conversions occur.

Together, children and youth make up about 20 percent of the American population. They have been aptly called "The World's Most Fruitful Field" in an article published by Child Evangelism Fellowship (CEF) some years ago.[1] The article reported on several surveys that found that 86 percent of Christians are converted to Christ by age fourteen, 10 percent between the ages of fifteen and thirty, and only 4 percent beyond the age of thirty. More recent surveys by the George Barna organization confirm that most conversions occur early in life.[2] His surveys found that about one-quarter of all Christian conversions occur between the ages of ten and twelve, roughly one-half between the ages of eight and thirteen, and about three-quarters by age eighteen. These surveys confirm that children and youth represent the most strategic generations in terms of evangelism. However, other data bring into question whether the church's role in addressing this strategic opportunity has been all that it might be. A survey of evangelical church Christian youth that was done some years back by Roy B. Zuck and Gene A. Getz found that only 28 percent of the churchgoing teens surveyed credited the church as the most important factor in their Christian conversion.[3] Parents were the most important for 29 percent, while programs and activities outside of the local church were rated most important by 36 percent. In a similar vein, more recent George Barna surveys indicate that only about 14 percent of Christian conversions are in response to a sermon.[4] About 38 percent are reported to be the result of family conversations or upbringing.

These findings concerning children and youth are significant. Although they represent only 20 percent of the American population, they account for roughly 75 percent of all Christian conversions. Yet 70 percent of the monies spent on evangelism by evangelical churches are directed toward adults.[5] If children and youth attend church at a level comparable to that of adults, which is reasonable to assume, then the church has an outreach opportunity to an estimated 60 percent of America's children and youth who are unchurched. The significance of this cannot be overemphasized in view of the high conversion rate among children and youth compared to that for adults. As suggested by the CEF article, they are indeed the world's most fruitful mission field.

Generation Y (the Millennial or youth generation)

Although Generation Y is still a "work in progress," important information about them is becoming available. Their future significance in terms of sheer numbers is in itself impressive. Figure 8-1 on the following page illustrates the annual birthrate trend for Americans since 1930.

The large birth bubble that occurred during the Boomer era and the subsequent decline when Xers entered the scene are generally well understood. What is sometimes not recognized is that the youth generation is in the process of forming a new birth bubble that will rival that of the Boomer generation, as shown in figure 8-1. This foretells that the youth of today will have a major influence over American society as they enter maturity and create a new age wave. Accordingly, the characteristics of this generation are of interest to the church, for it will one day minister to them as the adult population. Churches now seeking to expand their ministries to include an outreach to unchurched Boomers or Xers must take notice of Generation Y, since the children of the Boomers and Busters are part of the package.

Structuring a ministry to youth who come from unchurched backgrounds brings new challenges to tradition-oriented churches where the youth program has been geared primarily to Christian youth who have attended churches for most of their lives. Barna's surveys show that youth who are not Christians have a different perspective on many of life's

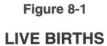

Figure 8-1

LIVE BIRTHS

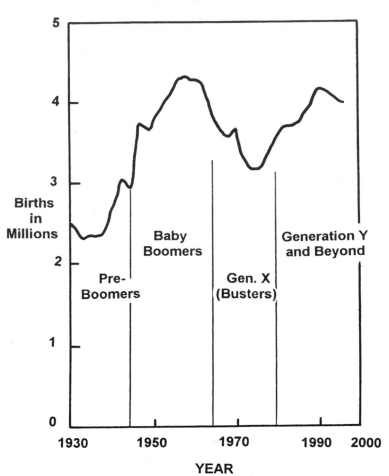

YEAR

Source: U.S. National Center for Health Statistics, *Vital Statistics of the U.S.*

issues than youth who have been raised in Christian families.[6] For example, only 55 percent of non-Christians (not born-again) subscribe to the view that God has established certain limits and that violating those limits has negative consequences. By way of contrast, 74 percent of the youth who describe themselves as born-again Christians subscribe to that view. Seventy-one percent of non-Christians view the purpose of life to be enjoyment and personal fulfillment, compared to 49 percent for Christian youth. Sixty-three percent of the non-Christian youth felt lying to be sometimes necessary, compared to 45 percent for Christians. Similarly, a higher percentage of the non-Christian youth surveyed subscribed to the views that there are no absolutes, that moral truth means different things to different people, that the Bible does not represent a reliable source for moral truth or practical standards for living, and that it is not totally accurate. These and many other findings demonstrate the differences that may be expected as youth not exposed to a Christian influence come into the church along with their parents.

While Generation Y is still a work in progress, those who have studied and worked with this generation observe certain emerging characteristics. These are summarized below and reflect a composite perspective compiled from a number of writings, with each characteristic having been identified by at least several of the writers reviewed.[7]

- *Collaborative.* Like Generation X, Generation Y appears to be more oriented toward collaboration than the Boomers. This sense of community extends beyond small groups to a larger segment of society. Millennials believe in the power of teamwork and cooperation and accordingly evidence less individualism than some earlier generations, all of which probably reflects the team-learning emphasis in public schools. The jury is still out on the effect this will have on individual achievement, which has been a cornerstone of America's technology and preeminence under capitalism and the high living standards it has produced. Collaboration has a collectivist ring to it that smacks of socialist philosophy, a system that has stifled individual incentive and proved to be a formula for national stagnation and economic decline.

- *Optimistic.* Unlike pessimistic Generation X, Generation Y is optimistic, upbeat, and conformist. They are neither rebellious nor materialistic, as were some of their forebears. Unlike the Xers who faced recessions, high unemployment, and stagnant careers, Generation Y has experienced the high economic growth rate, low unemployment, and general prosperity of the 1990s. They look forward to the future with positive expectations and assume that jobs and good income will be available. They foresee a better economic environment in the future than what existed for their parents, and many look forward to a family situation in which one parent will be able to remain at home to raise the children. Most feel strongly that their families will be more important and take precedence over money and careers.

- *Spiritual.* Generation Y is expected to be more open to the church than Xers. However, as postmodernists they are open to all religious persuasions and have a pick-and-mix attitude. A big question in their minds is why Christianity is the only way to God. Millennials appear to have a sense of expectancy that God will be doing something new in their generation.

- *Tolerant.* Steeped in postmodernist philosophy, Millennials are tolerant of all views but one: intolerance. To be tolerant means that no view can be imposed on anyone else. They largely reject any institution or religion claiming to have a corner on the truth. A major challenge to the church will be how to convey effectively the absolute truths of Christianity to this generation.

- *Protected or favored.* Older generations seem committed to protect Generation Y. This protection is evidenced by legislation to protect children's rights, the emphasis on new child-safety standards, and the sometimes overprotective manner of parents. Although working parents are still the dominant trend, they increasingly indicate that more time with their families is more important than more pay. Perhaps in reaction to their experience, parents of Generation Y want their children to stay children and not be rushed prematurely into adult experiences and responsibilities.

Social trends, in general, are shifting away from child neglect toward protection and support. Many churches now teach parenting classes, and organizations like Focus on the Family and Families Northwest of Bellevue, Washington, provide a variety of programs and literature designed to help stabilize families and marriages. The fact that this generation has become virtually "untouchable" has a negative consequence for church youth ministries. Much-needed volunteers are hard to come by; many stay away out of fear of legal consequences by suspicious parents, the runaway litigation frenzy that now engulfs almost every aspect of society, and the serious consequences of false allegations.

- *Relativist.* Postmodernism has left Generation Y in a moral vacuum. Millennials do not recognize universal rights and wrongs; in their mind set, absolutes do not exist. Rather, moral guidelines depend upon situations, circumstances, and community.

    Some observers believe there is evidence of a sexual counter-revolution, although such data is not conclusive. Having seen the devastation of divorce and the consequences of disease and pregnancy that occur when unmarried teens unprepared for parenthood have sexual relationships, Generation Y may be rejecting the complete sexual freedom advocated by preceding generations. Unfortunately, much of this concern translates only into a more conscientious use of contraceptives and an attitude of waiting for sex until, not marriage, but finding a potential marriage partner. It is important that young people see morality being lived out in both how we behave and how we respond to immorality. If it hopes to influence youth on this issue, the Christian community will need to stop its withdrawal and retreat from the political process by challenging political correctness (community-dictated values) when it conflicts with biblical morality, attending school board meetings in greater numbers, and organizing to provide a collective voice that cannot be ignored.

- *Cyberliterate.* Millennials represent a computer-oriented generation that is increasingly drawn to interactive, as opposed to linear, forms of receiving information. Television, movies, radio, newspapers, books, and other traditional media are essentially linear; that is, information is received from providers in a one-way flow. The increasingly interactive forms provide a new opportunity and avenue through which to minister. Online ministries are growing in numbers, and chat rooms are expected to become a common mode of

communication. The downside, of course, is that anyone can go online, and checking the credibility or credentials of those utilizing
this new media is difficult, if not impossible.

Generation Y is like the Boomers in some respects, more like Generation X in others, and uniquely different from either in still others.
Like the Boomers, they are optimistic and confident, are the beneficia-
ries of being raised in a youth-friendly environment, and are generally
supportive of establishment institutions. Like the Xers, they are totally indoctrinated in postmodernist philosophy, are much more family friendly,
more spiritually sensitive, and less obsessed with careers and materialistic
fulfillment than the Boomers. Like both the Boomers and Xers, Millennials are largely tolerant of all views, including religious ones. And like both
of the preceding generations, Millennials recognize no absolute rights
and wrongs. Unlike either, they are oriented toward collaboration and
teamwork in virtually all areas of life, as opposed to an individualistic
approach, and may be undergoing a sexual counterrevolution.

These findings suggest that some adjustments to the tradition-oriented
church's approach to youth ministry will have to be made. Barna suggests
that churches adopt a firm but interactive style with a discussion approach
that enables teens to feel they have a stake in the outcome or proceedings.
Millennials resist imposed standards in which they do not have an input.
Leader accessibility is also particularly important. Being available to the
teens and becoming involved in their lives bring the leaders credibility
and the opportunity to exert a positive influence. Effective leadership also
requires befriending them, providing encouragement, and helping them
with their real-life problems. As confidence and trust develop, youth leaders earn the right to introduce them to serious Christianity and provide
positive lifestyle alternatives.

Children

Since children have not yet taken on a cultural "set," we do not discuss
them in that context. However, children can be receptive to the gospel
and present possible ministry opportunities, particularly to Caretaker
churches. These churches are singled out in this context since most do not
have an effective outreach component in their ministries. An outreach to

children is one way this void can be filled. Moreover, most churches can implement it without disrupting their current ministries.

Within a very short time span, Caretaker churches can implement a program of evangelism directed toward unchurched children. This remarkably simple program, which often has rather dramatic results, involves the formation of church-sponsored Good News Clubs. These children's Bible clubs, which meet in homes once a week, are a ministry of Child Evangelism Fellowship, Inc. (CEF), which functions as a service organization, providing lesson materials, visual aids, and teacher training. The church provides the host and teachers for each club. Teacher training usually takes place at weekly meetings conducted by CEF at local offices in most cities. Since teachers receive instruction and help as needed concerning the lesson of the week, they do not need to attend a long preparatory indoctrination program.

The Good News Club program is well suited for Caretaker churches in that the significant proportion of seniors in such churches usually includes a number who are able and willing to become involved and do not have substantial other commitments. Most are experienced and understanding concerning children since they have raised their own. Moreover, seniors, who represent one of the most underutilized resources in the church today, have the time flexibility in retirement to hold club meetings at times convenient for children to attend. Experience demonstrates that it is not unusual to have ten to twenty clubs in operation within a few months after such a program is launched. With each typical club attendance at ten or more children, a church can achieve a weekly outreach to a hundred or more unchurched children, one that likely approaches the size of many small Caretaker church Sunday school programs.

Children are extremely responsive to the gospel, and CEF data confirms that a high rate of Christian conversions occur at club meetings. Obviously, staffing the Good News Club program with teachers and hosts is not limited to seniors. It is also well suited to stay-at-home men and women of any age. In fact, those with children make particularly good hosts since their children can be most effective in inviting other neighborhood children with whom they play to attend the club meetings. Parents feel secure in letting their children attend such a program in the home of a neighbor they know, respect, and trust.

The Caretaker church is probably better suited for outreach ministries such as Good News Clubs than generation driven churches that are primarily focused on a specific generational category, such as Xers or Boomers. The program would fill a large ministry void that presently exists in churches, since very few have outreach ministries to unchurched children, in spite of the fact that statistics confirm that children represent one of the best evangelistic opportunities of our day. Offering such a program would also inject a new sense of life and purpose into Caretaker churches, even if other approaches to unchurched Baby Boomers and Xers are determined to be inappropriate. For more information on the Good News Club program and other ministries of CEF, call them at (313) 456-4321 or write to Child Evangelism Fellowship, Inc., P.O. Box 348, Warrenton, MO 63383-0348. Online see *www.gospelcom.net/cef.*

Chapter nine

PREPARING FOR CHANGE

LAUNCHING A NEW MINISTRY OUTREACH targeting unchurched Boomers or Xers involves major changes. Churches must precede these with appropriate preparation if the outreach is to succeed. The required preparation is largely educational and should be directed toward both the church leadership and the congregation. Most Caretaker and other long-established traditional churches become inward focused and increasingly dedicated to survival for the sake of themselves.[1] At best, some leaders and members of these churches have a vague understanding of post-modernism, while most have no understanding at all. Nor do most generally recognize that today's society consists of generation based multiculturalism in which each of the major adult generations — Pre-Boomers, Boomers, and Xers — are culturally so different from one another that a different approach to ministry is required for each.

The preparation needed prior to instituting major change is that which brings both the leadership and the congregation back to basics, namely, a re-examination of what the church is here for. Such introspection by the church to determine if change is necessary to bring the church back to the fulfillment of basic purposes and the nature of such change should be initiated and endorsed by the pastor. Without strong pastoral leadership in this regard, change is a dead issue. The church board must also become involved and take the lead in the planning and decision process. If the effort is to succeed, it must reach strong, if not unanimous, agreement to proceed. Finally, the congregation must be sold on the plan. This educational process can probably best be accomplished with the congregation through a sermon series, while an appropriately structured weekend retreat or workshop for the leaders can be helpful. Unless proposed major change is couched in such a context, namely, the fundamental purposes of the church and an assessment of where it stands in fulfilling such purposes, substantial controversy and opposition are virtually assured. Any major change will bring some controversy anyway, but the objective is to so manage the change process that it is minimal.

Definition of terms

At this point it would probably be helpful to review the intent of certain terms used. "Traditional churches" continues to refer to churches in which the approach to and format of ministry remain largely unchanged from that which existed before the Boomers ushered in postmodernism and related cultural changes. While traditional church congregations are multigenerational, they are composed almost entirely of long-established churchgoing Christians and their families. As such, they represent a distinct cultural category in themselves, which we'll refer to as the "traditional Christian culture." The generational categories that constitute this culture enjoy a Christ-centered cultural continuity that transcends other generational characteristics and influences. Reference to Boomers and Generation Xers in this chapter applies to those who are not a part of this traditional Christian culture. Rather, they are the unchurched and generally non-Christian Boomers and Xers.

Purposes

Willingness to accept change begins with a vision of what the church is here for and where it wants to go in terms of goals. This, in turn, begins with a definition of its purposes. Unfortunately, most churches do not define purposes in specific terms, and those that do rarely emphasize them or make an objective periodic assessment as to whether or not they are being fulfilled. Churches that do emphasize purposes most often do not distinguish between the personal versus the institutional aspects. The personal application of defined purposes applies to individuals and is largely a function of lifestyle, while the institutional application translates into church programs. Both types of purposes are important, and it is a mistake to either institutionalize or to personalize them. Purposes are fulfilled as both personal and institutional aspects are implemented synergistically. However, since this book is on church ministries, we are focusing primarily on the institutional aspect.

Preaching about purposes apart from the personal/institutional distinction gets the church leadership off the hook because it throws the entire obligation for fulfillment of purposes on the backs of individuals. It invokes the old cliché that the church is really a training center that equips and prepares Christians to go out into the world to do spiritual battle and make a difference. But such preaching ignores the reality that certain aspects of purpose fulfillment are achievable only through collective effort in the form of institutional programs. Personalizing all purposes to the exclusion of the institutional application also eliminates meaningful accountability. Personal performance in terms of fulfilling basic purposes cannot be measured. Fulfillment of purposes from an institutional perspective, however, is measurable and should be, with the church leadership holding itself accountable for the results.

So, while the obligation of individual Christians to bear spiritual fruit through their personal lives is very relevant, it is only one aspect of fulfilling the purposes of the church. Equally important are the role of the church as an institution and the extent to which its programs contribute to the fulfillment of these purposes. To illustrate, equipping the saints to be the salt and light of the world is an institutional role of the church that fulfills the purpose of discipleship, but the church does not fulfill the purpose of evangelism in this instance even though it may be indirectly influencing personal evangelism to take place through the lives of its members. Sunday school instruction, training in personal evangelism, or other mentoring ministries may ultimately result in personal evangelism through the witness of the individuals trained or discipled, however, the direct purpose being fulfilled by the church through such programs is nevertheless discipleship. An example of institutional evangelism, on the other hand, is a church-sponsored Good News Club program, attended largely by unchurched children, through which children respond to the gospel presentations and invitation to receive Christ as their personal Savior. Or, an evangelistic outreach might be a men's breakfast program to which unchurched men are invited to hear a sports celebrity or some other featured speaker, all of which is designed to present a strong Christian witness and evangelistic challenge.

Under a more comprehensive plan of action, fulfilling the purpose of evangelism would likely involve the launch of what has commonly become referred to as a "seeker-sensitive service." In his book *The Purpose Driven Church*, Rick Warren describes this approach in depth.[2] Seeker services are evangelistic in emphasis and complement personal evangelism. They provide a group witness that reinforces and confirms the personal witness of the friend who brought the visitor to the church.

The phrase "seeker-sensitive" implies a variety of actions and preparations designed to make the church experience as "comfortable" as possible for the unchurched visitor. These might entail convenient parking, warm welcoming techniques, a fast-moving service, and a myriad of other such provisions. Such actions and preparations are a key to attracting large numbers of unchurched postmodernists into a church setting and ultimately to faith in Christ through the messages and other ministries of the church.

We've referred to evangelism and discipleship, but these are only two of several important purposes of the church as an institution. There is plenty of room for disagreement as to what biblically constitutes purposes of the church. Most, however, would not take too much exception to a list that includes the following:

1. Worship

2. Discipleship or disciple building

3. Evangelism

4. Mutual support and encouragement of the local body of believers

5. Community support and outreach

This last purpose might appear to duplicate evangelism. What is intended, however, is outreach in the sense of showing compassion and help concerning the needs of those in the community who are not a part of the local church body. We're admonished to love our neighbors as ourselves (Matt. 22:39). Real Life Church of Maple Valley, Washington, is a good example of a church that includes this as a part of its ministry philosophy. This church, oriented to Generation X, has grown rapidly since it was launched a few years ago, in part because of its good community relations and outreach. Typical projects in this regard include

- periodic auto-maintenance days, when volunteers perform routine automotive maintenance for single moms;

- bicycle days, when kids can get their bikes repaired free or, if needed, receive a reconditioned one made available from unclaimed police inventories;

- a youth center called Unplugged, where high schoolers and junior highers from the community are welcome to drop in on Friday

Figure 9-1

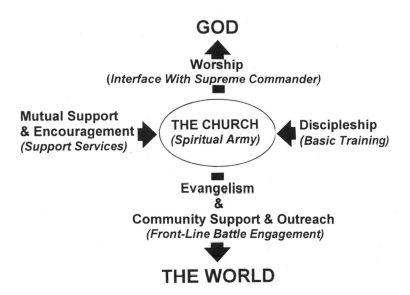

PURPOSES

GOD

Worship
(Interface With Supreme Commander)

**Mutual Support
& Encouragement**
(Support Services)

THE CHURCH
(Spiritual Army)

Discipleship
(Basic Training)

**Evangelism
&
Community Support & Outreach**
(Front-Line Battle Engagement)

THE WORLD

Note: The wording in parentheses and italics puts the
purposes in military parlance from the perspective of
spiritual warfare

evenings for a safe and enjoyable time of recreation (pool, games, snacks), hearing a Christian musical group, or just talking to a Christian youth leader; and

• participation with several other churches in the operation of a low-rent transitional housing facility for single moms facing difficult circumstances.

Note that the five listed purposes are either oriented inward toward the church or oriented outward from the church, as illustrated in figure 9-1. Worship, evangelism, and community support and outreach are all outward oriented. Discipleship and mutual support and encouragement, on the other hand, are inward oriented. Equating the church to a spiritual army makes it apparent that two of these outward-oriented purposes — evangelism and community support and outreach — are really what the church is here for. They define the church mission. Apart from such outreach to convey the Christian message to the world there is no reason for the earthly church to exist. Worship, the other outward-oriented purpose, is directed toward God and is essential since it provides the vital link to the Supreme Commander. Worship, of course, is essential to a healthy spiritual relationship between believers and the Divine in any context, but it seems unlikely that God has left believers on earth primarily for the purpose of worship. True worship could more effectively be accomplished in heaven, free from the distractions, worries, and influences that impede optimum worship.

The inward-oriented purposes (discipleship, mutual support and encouragement) are no less essential since they equip believers to carry out the outreach purposes that represent the primary mission of the church. In military parlance, these are equivalent to basic training (discipleship) and maintenance of the support services and supply lines (mutual support and encouragement) so essential to maintaining the troops in battle-ready condition in order to carry out frontline battle assignments (outreach-oriented purposes).

So, while all of these purposes are of equal importance and are mutually interdependent, effective outreach largely defines whether the church is fulfilling its basic mission. A church that focuses upon discipleship and mutual support and encouragement (i.e., much good fellowship, Bible study, doctrinal teaching, etc.) but fails to demonstrate an effective outreach to the community cannot realistically be regarded as a spiritually healthy church, regardless of size or level of attendance. Unfortunately, such an inward focus characterizes many Caretaker churches today.

Some churches would be quick to include other purposes in addition to those mentioned in the preceding discussion, such as missions. The support of missions and other parachurch organizations is really fulfilling previously outlined purposes by proxy. It does this by substituting capital for other church program resources. The selection of such organizations based on their focus and agenda determines the local church purposes fulfilled by such support. Short-term mission teams or missionaries that are sent out and administered by the church do not fall under the by-proxy category. Nevertheless, they too are fulfilling evangelism, discipleship, or other defined purposes of the church. Missions, therefore, is a program to accomplish purposes rather than a purpose in itself. Our intent is not to dwell further on this list of purposes or its possible variations. The important point is that each church ought to have a well-thought-out and definitive statement of its purposes, or the reason for which it exists, in a word, the *what* of the church — what it is here for.

However, the *what* is only one dimension of purposes. The other dimension is *to whom*. Who are the objects of these purposes? There are a number of possible ways to categorize people to whom purposes apply. Generational categories, which are largely a function of age and cultural orientation, is believed to be the best way since each generational category consists of people with common characteristics that, in turn, determine the nature of appropriate church programming. The major categories in this regard are those discussed in preceding chapters, namely, children, Generation Y, Generation X, Baby Boomers, and Pre-Boomers.

To illustrate the two-dimensional aspect of purposes, consider evangelism, one of the reasons for which the church exists. In fulfilling this purpose as an institution, the church must tailor programs suited to the intended object. The programs will be different for Pre-Boomers, Boomers, Xers, youth, and children. Taking into account resource constraints and where the church can best utilize available resources for evangelistic outreach, it must decide which generational categories (the *to whom* dimension) will be its focus. A church might decide to implement evangelism programs directed toward children and Generation Y as the most urgent priorities, while deferring programming to other generational categories until additional resources become available or until other higher priority needs are satisfied.

Figure 9-2 illustrates conceptually the Ministries Matrix concept from a ministries management system described in *Church Wake-Up Call.*[5] The chart demonstrates graphically the two-dimensional aspect of purposes. The basic purposes are represented by numbers on the left-hand side of the chart (the *what*) and the generational categories (the *to whom*) are represented across the top by letters. The squares formed where the purposes (horizontal arrows) and the generational categories (vertical arrows) intersect are called ministry categories. Under this management system, each of these ministry categories is prioritized by the church leadership. Once this is done, the actual ministries or programs of the church are listed

Figure 9-2

DEFINING THE CHURCH MISSION

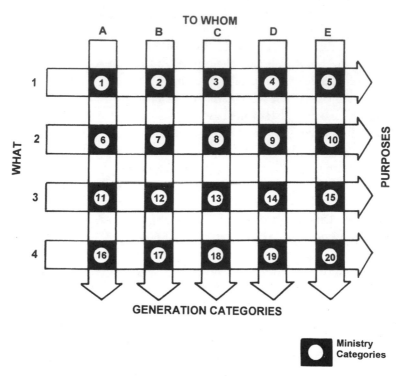

according to where they best fit in these ministry categories. When and if the actual programming is revealed to be out of sync with the priorities defined for each ministry category (purposes by generational category) by this process, appropriate changes in the ministries or program agenda are made.

Figure 9-3 uses this Ministries Matrix concept to convey the current ministries emphasis of a typical Caretaker church compared to how it would probably prioritize each ministry category. We suggest using this type of display as a technique to analyze and convey the probable disparity between defined purposes, priorities, and actual ministry em-

Figure 9-3

EVALUATING CHURCH MISSION
VS. PROGRAMMING

PURPOSES OF LOCAL CHURCH				
WHAT **TO WHOM**	**TRADITIONAL CHRISTIAN CULTURE**	**UNCHURCHED**		
		GENERATION X	**BOOMERS**	**PRE-BOOMERS**
WORSHIP	●	W ● *Problem*	●	○
EVANGELISM	W ○	W ● *Problem*	W ● *Problem*	○
DISCIPLESHIP	●	W ● *Problem*	●	○
MUTUAL SUPPORT & ENCOURAGEMENT	●	W ● *Problem*	●	○
COMMUNITY OUTREACH & SUPPORT	W ○	W ● *Problem*	W ○	W ○

● High Priority   W: Weak or no programming
○ Low Priority

phasis as part of the process for preparing the church leadership, and ultimately the congregation, for change. The purposes to which most Caretaker churches subscribe are not being accommodated by their current ministries approach. The gaping voids revealed in figure 9-3 in terms of programming to unchurched Boomers and Generation Xers, which most believers would see as high-priority outreach targets, should help influence attitudes and receptivity to the strategies outlined in the next chapter.

The educational process in preparing for change would obviously consist of much more than a Ministries Matrix analysis. A suggested message series might include the following subjects:

1. Postmodernism — What Is it?
2. Today's Generation Based Multiculturalism and Its Implications for the Church
3. Who Are the Baby Boomers?
4. Who Are Generation Xers?
5. Who Are Today's Youth?
6. Purposes of the Church
7. Prioritized Purposes versus Current Programming
8. New Outreach Strategies and Goals

Not coincidentally, this outline follows quite closely the material covered in this book. The information contained should therefore be a useful resource for developing such a message series. Similarly, the figures included throughout this book are intended for reproduction and use to the extent that they are deemed helpful.

Transfer growth

Important preparation for any of the strategies outlined in the next chapter includes an adequate base from which to launch a new outreach ministry. This is particularly true for strategies involving the addition of generationally segmented services and supporting programs. The current ministry base in terms of membership and financial resources must be strong enough to accommodate possible staff additions and layperson support of new programs. Although there are strategy options described in the next chapter to accommodate different church situations, the first order of business for any Caretaker church seeking to launch a new outreach ministry is to ensure that it has in place procedures and programs that will optimize growth of its current tradition-oriented ministries base.

For most Caretaker churches this means transfer growth — growth from other believers moving into the area or seeking to make a change in churches for some other reason. Although transfer growth is not real growth, and is therefore frowned upon by many church-growth authorities, it has its place. Many small churches are going nowhere. Each year three thousand to five thousand close their doors for the last time and become extinct, according to Charles Arn.[4] Accordingly, some consolidation of membership among Caretaker churches to provide the critical mass needed by those with an outreach vision is beneficial from the perspective of the church universal. By *critical mass* is meant a congregational size sufficiently large to provide the human and financial resources to launch a new outreach ministry targeting unchurched Boomers or Xers. This refers not only to a second worship service but also to the ancillary programs necessary for a balanced ministry. This is particularly important since a second worship service could reduce attendance at the present service by 25 to 30 percent.[5]

Unfortunately, many Caretaker churches are so inward oriented that they do not even do a good job at transfer growth. Therefore, it's not a bad idea to review transfer-growth procedures and to institute changes if needed before embarking on an expanded outreach targeting a different generational segment. Many Caretaker churches are friendly churches, while at the same time being churches where it is difficult to make friends. People want the latter. Critical to good transfer growth is a well-administered small-group fellowship program that systematically brings together newcomers and current church members at home potlucks once a month or so, where they can intermingle and get acquainted. The attendance should be shuffled so that newcomers are exposed to different members each time. Other approaches may also be structured that integrate newcomers into the church fellowship as quickly as possible. What's important is that the church must make a managed effort to assure that this occurs. It probably requires a small committee dedicated to scheduling these potlucks, inviting those who attend each, assuring that the mix of newcomers and present members changes each time, and maintaining records on church visitors and retention rates. Without such an organized effort, many visitors will come for a time but then drop out after feeling that they are not getting to know people or becoming integrated into what often is somewhat of a closed community of close-knit members who are more interested in long-established relationships than in opening their circles to newcomers. This committee should comprise individuals who represent a broad adult age range and who are familiar with most of the congregation members. This assures that some, if not most, of the members invited to attend the potlucks are in the same age bracket as the visitors who are invited to attend.

Capacity expansion

When the attendance at worship services exceeds 80 to 85 percent of seating capacity, it is usually time to consider the launch of a second morning worship service, assuming that one does not already exist. Arn concludes that attendance maintained at such levels for more than four consecutive months indicates saturation of current capacity after which further growth is highly improbable.[6] Assuming that the church is still not sufficiently large or financially capable of supporting a new generation driven outreach targeting unchurched postmodern generations, a second service becomes essential in terms of building church size and financial strength to permit such strategy.

Two second-service options or strategies are available in this context. One is a second service that duplicates the first. The other is a second service that, although not generation driven, is more seeker sensitive and evangelistic in format than the first. As such, it would be a service to which regular attendees are encouraged to invite unchurched non-Christian friends. It would enhance prospects for conversion growth and avoid the mistake described by Warren in *The Purpose Driven Church* that most churches make of trying to evangelize the lost and edify believers in the same service.[7] At Saddleback, where Warren is senior pastor, believer services are held Wednesday evenings, while seeker services are held on Saturday evenings and Sunday mornings.

Although the first option, launching a second service that duplicates the first, does not incorporate this outreach advantage, it does satisfy the requirement of providing for additional capacity. It also requires less preparation on the part of the pastoral staff and worship team since the two services are identical. While it does not provide the same conversion growth potential as the second option, other ways exist to partially accommodate this concern. One is to designate one service each month as seeker sensitive and evangelism oriented, as opposed to believer and edification oriented. For example, the first service of each month might be so designated, and the congregation encouraged to invite unchurched non-Christian friends to these services. This, of course, could be done and probably should be, even if there is only one worship service. While not the optimal outreach approach to unchurched postmodern generational groups, it would foster some level of conversion growth while the church is posturing itself for a more aggressive outreach strategy.

Summing it up, it's essential for the Caretaker church to be properly postured before launching a new outreach ministry directed toward one or more of the postmodern-oriented generational groups. This translates into assuring the existence of an adequate launch base in terms of financial and human resources. Launching prematurely is a formula for failure and can have a demoralizing impact on the congregation. Such posturing requires well-defined goals and an organized plan of action that embodies the key elements described in preceding paragraphs to cause it to happen.

Chapter ten

ALTERNATIVE OUTREACH MODELS

IN VIEW OF THE DIFFERENT CULTURAL CHARACTERISTICS of each generational category, how do Caretaker churches, those that we've defined as steeped in traditional Christian culture, adapt their ministries to reach out to unchurched Boomers and Generation Xers? Some take the position that they don't. That is, they don't attempt to adapt current ministries into some kind of a modified one-size-fits-all blend. The cultural differences are considered too great under this view, particularly concerning worship services but also with respect to related ancillary ministries. Figure 10-1 illustrates this point by highlighting the differences that must be accommodated concerning various aspects of ministry for the traditional-Christian-culture church compared with churches designed to attract unchurched Boomers and Generation Xers. This information reflects the earlier discussion of chapters 4 through 7. These differences lead to solutions that embody some variation of what thousands of churches across the country are doing, namely, establishing separate worship services, as well as other generation driven ministries, to accommodate today's generation based cultural diversity. This is commonly referred to as a "church-within-a-church" strategy or formula.

Others, however, believe that it is possible to blend classic church traditions with elements of contemporary worship. Greg Warner, executive editor of *Faith Works*, highlights these views in a recent article and refers to Robert Webber of Wheaton University as a strong advocate of a blended approach.[1] Webber teaches a workshop at Wheaton on this subject.

The preponderance of evidence, however, seems to indicate that generationally segmented worship may be the best strategy for reaching today's unchurched masses. Charles Arn supports this view and has found that 80 percent of the churches that establish a second-service approach achieve increases in attendance, contributions, and conversions.[2] He estimates that half of the country's churches would benefit by a second service, which is a very significant statistic in light of findings that an estimated three-fourths of America's churches are plateaued or declining. Arn's

Figure 10-1

MINISTRY IMPLICATIONS

Aspect	Christian Culture	Boomers	Gen Xers
Congregation	Mostly Believers	Spiritual Seekers	

Message	• Exposition
	• Exhortation
	• Proclamation
	  Evangelism
	• Dogmatic
		• How-to
		• Life Issues
		• Application of
		  Biblical Principles
			• Creative
			  Storytelling
			• Narrative
			  Evangelism
			• Relational

Worship Format	• Traditional
	• Semiformal
		• Contemporary
		• Informal
		• Charismatic or
		  Experiential
			• Contemporary
			• Informal
			• Videos/Film Clips
			• Skits
			• Audience
			  Involvement
			• Celebration

Music	• Traditional and
	  Contemporary
	  Balance
		• Contemporary	• Contemporary

Institutional Loyalty	• High	• Low	• Low
Membership	• Emphasize	• Deemphasize	• Deemphasize

Involvement	• High	• Selective
		• Low
		  Commitment
			• Want to Be
			  Involved

Small Groups	• Program-
	  Oriented
		• Support-
		  Oriented
			• Relationship-
			  Oriented

Primary Leadership	• Married Males	• Equal Participation by Singles and Women Expected	
Adult Social Focus	• Married Couples and Families	• Equal Focus on Singles	
Evangelism Type or Method	• Proclamation • Personal	• Personal • Proclamation	• Narrative • Friendship • Socratic • Process
Evangelism Vehicle	• Messages • Crusades • Individuals	• Support Groups • Individuals • Messages	• Relational Small Groups • Messages

book, *How to Start a New Service* (Baker Books, 1997), is highly recommended for any church contemplating a second service, and we have drawn heavily upon his research in this chapter.

Arn also believes that church size is not a serious constraint to beginning a new service, with fifty people at the current service representing the attendance level below which a second service is not advisable. Our personal observation is that very few Caretaker churches have actually ventured into a second service without a much larger current service attendance than this lower boundary level. Moreover, a distinction is important as to whether the second service is oriented toward the same generational mix as the first in order to accommodate overcrowding or provide schedule options, as opposed to targeting an entirely different generational category, such as unchurched Boomers or Xers. In the latter case, there is much more to such an outreach than a second worship service, as indicated in chapters 5 and 7.

Arn's conclusions concerning church size and second worship services provide a very optimistic outlook for Caretaker churches interested in the church-within-a-church approach. As mentioned in chapter 1, about half of all Protestant churches in America are attended by fewer than a hundred worshipers. Less than 3 percent have an average attendance of a thousand or more. With this relatively small number of large churches, the primary challenge to reach unchurched younger generations falls to the much larger number of small to midsize churches. If Caretaker churches fail to respond to this challenge, new start-up churches will fulfill the ministry void by reason of default. As touched upon in chapter 3, Caretaker churches are much better postured to meet this need than start-up churches, for the former have in-place facilities, an experienced administrative structure, youth and children programs, and a talent pool of laypersons to draw upon for the core personnel of new programs. In spite of such advantages, many Caretaker churches sit on the sidelines, stagnating and heading for extinction, while new churches are springing up throughout the country, starting from scratch to carve out ministries to a spiritually receptive but unchurched segment of America. It boils down to vision, motivation, and leadership to impart such a vision to congregations.

Apart from these considerations, few small to midsize Caretaker churches have the resources to launch segmented services to accommodate all of the generation based cultural categories discussed throughout this book. This leaves two basic options. One is a more selective approach. Although the typical Caretaker church cannot structure separate ministries to every generational category, many can move beyond their current traditional Christian culture to add an outreach to either unchurched Boomers or Generation Xers. The remaining option, if this is not feasible, is a blended approach until such time that a more aggressive strategy is possible.

Listed below are five outreach models or strategies suggested for Caretaker churches. These are designed to accommodate varying circumstances in terms of size, resources, and congregational attitudes.

- Model 1: Boomer-Friendly Blended Services
- Model 2: Church within a Church
- Model 3: Two Churches in One
- Model 4: Foster Church
- Model 5: Church Planting

The objective of each of these strategies is to draw unchurched non-Christians into the church, evangelize them, and then lead them to successively deeper levels of spiritual maturity and commitment. Though the objective sounds simple, we often lose sight of these fundamental essentials that are not dissimilar from those of the business world, although the product is different. At one point one of the authors was employed by the Welch Grape Juice Company, a firm that processed grapes into a variety of grape-based products, including juice, jam, jelly, and wine. Grapes were the raw material central to all of the sophisticated manufacturing processes that converted them into these end products. Without grapes there would be no reason for the processing plant to exist. Unchurched nonbelievers are to the church what grapes are to the grape processing plant. If unchurched non-Christians are not drawn into the church on a consistent basis for "processing," it is questionable whether all of the other church programs and organizational schemes that are currently in vogue are relevant.

Unfortunately, this central element of unchurched non-Christians is often almost nonexistent in many small to midsize churches. Typically, there are plenty of programs to process and reprocess believers, but very little influx in the way of unchurched seekers. Although programming that processes believers to successively deeper levels of spiritual maturity and commitment (the "end products" of church processing) is essential following conversion, churches today must direct more emphasis toward the missing link — attracting the unchurched into our churches and evangelizing them. In order for this to happen, an essential requirement is a generation driven focus tailored to accommodate the unique cultural characteristics of targeted generational groups. Otherwise, they will not be tuned in to what the church has to say. Another requirement is programming that includes a strong seeker-sensitive and evangelistic emphasis. Outreach to unchurched nonbelievers must emphasize the basic gospel message, as opposed to edification and the exposition of doctrinal subtleties concerning which they are neither receptive nor spiritually ready to assimilate. An additional component is the individual involvement of congregational members in bringing unchurched friends to attend programs that are designed to reach them in a nonthreatening program format.

We cannot overemphasize this last point. While the primary thrust of this book is on church programming that provides the proper setting for outreach, most people who attend church for the first time come because they are invited by a friend or relative. Notice that they were invited, not evangelized. Very few people have the gift of evangelism. Unfortunately, churches often put a guilt trip on members for their failure to evangelize unchurched friends through a personal witness. Since most people are inept at this and since many churches lack programming specifically designed to reach unchurched seekers who visit, little evangelism takes place.

Larry Gilbert, in *How to Influence Your Loved Ones for Christ When You Don't Have the Gift of Evangelism*, advocates the concept of team evangelism.[3] Research confirms that only 10 percent of church members have the spiritual gift of evangelism. Under team evangelism, the 90 percent of Christians who do not have this gift are encouraged to use the spiritual gifts that they do have in establishing relationships that exert a positive spiritual influence and foster a receptiveness on the part of friends to accept invitations to visit church. The church, as a body of individual believers in which the diverse gifts of the body are knit together synergistically into an integrated whole, can fulfill the evangelism function corporately through well-designed programming. The role of the individual and the role of the church as a corporate body are therefore complementary, both being essential for effective outreach to take place. Gilbert's book on team evangelism is highly recommended as a source for training individual church members in their role under this concept and is well suited for an adult Sunday school classes curriculum. It includes a survey form that enables readers to determine their spiritual gifts.

Model 1: Boomer-friendly blended services

A suboptimum strategy suggested only for churches unable to pursue some variation of models 2 or 3, model 1 has a more restricted application. It holds promise for reaching some unchurched Boomers but not Generation Xers. Boomers are now maturing to middle age (thirty-seven to fifty-six years of age in 2001), and the traditional Christian culture has mellowed in its attitude toward contemporary worship. In short, these two cultures have drifted closer together and, with the moderating influence of time, have become mutually more tolerant. Boomers are also now more accepting of the tradition-oriented church because their children need some type of moral grounding. Further, as Pre-Boomers age and gradually decline as a percentage of the total population, those churchgoers of the Boomer and younger generations are increasing as a percentage of Caretaker church attendance. Although these younger attendees embrace the traditional Christian culture, they are more in tune with unchurched Boomers than are the Pre-Boomers.

Blending does not work with Generation Xers, however. They are sufficiently different culturally from both the Boomers and the traditional Christian culture as to make a blending attempt like mixing oil with water. Anyone who has attended a Generation X church service recognizes the incompatibility. When Dieter Zander left New Song Church to take responsibility for the Generation X ministry at Willow Creek, he found it necessary to establish a service that was separate and different from the approach so successful in reaching Boomers there. If Xers could not be blended with Boomers, a culture with which they are much more in tune philosophically, attempting to blend them with a traditional Christian culture would prove futile.

Blended worship services involving Boomers in a traditional Caretaker church means accepting a number of changes. Under a blended approach there would have to be considerable compromise from an approach designed for Boomers alone (see chap. 5). And while some Boomers may not find a blended approach satisfactory in meeting their needs, Boomers are not all alike. Others would fit into such a format quite nicely. Musically, the blended worship service would involve more contemporary music, more praise choruses, fewer hymns, and an instrumental group or orchestra largely replacing the organ. The sermon emphasis would need to change to more "how-to" messages relevant to the daily issues of life. Another change would probably be opening the doors of involvement and leadership more widely to singles and women. And the church might need to introduce more small support-group ministries oriented to various types of dysfunctionality and problems (marital, addiction, divorce recovery, single parenting, etc.). In general, the traditional ministry style would have to become more Boomer friendly. Many tradition-oriented congregations can be quite accepting of such changes if properly prepared, as discussed in the preceding chapter. Others may find such changes difficult or unacceptable.

If there are two morning worship services to accommodate attendance levels, an approach worth considering is to structure one to be seeker sensitive and evangelism oriented, while the other remains believer and edification oriented. In the case of a single worship service, consider having one service each month designated for a seeker-sensitive evangelism emphasis and encourage church members to invite newcomers and unchurched friends to these services.

Model 2: Church within a church

The most common approach in establishing an outreach to unchurched Boomers or Xers involves a second contemporary service and ministry under a church-within-a-church model. Both the traditional and the contemporary ministries fall under the jurisdiction and oversight of the senior pastor under this approach. An assistant pastor or other staff person provides overall coordination of the new ministry, but the senior pastor delivers the message at both services and is in overall control. The service formats differ, being tailored appropriately to each generation based cultural category.

While the same basic message is presented at each service, the contemporary service can be modified somewhat to accommodate a seeker-sensitive or evangelistic emphasis, as well as the cultural characteristics of the group. Traditional congregations usually adapt well to the preaching style to which Boomers or Xers respond, but the reverse is not usually true. This is not to imply a watering down or compromise of basic truths in the message, but it may be necessary to repackage it in ways that communicate more effectively to Boomers or Generation Xers. Sermons steeped in reasoned arguments do not resonate with Xers, but sermons take on meaning when packaged in a story context that conveys the same truth. Similarly, Boomers respond to messages related to issues in their personal lives. However, we do not want to overstate the difference in how various generational categories respond to preaching style.

Relatively modest adaptation in the same message delivered to each generational group may well be adequate. For example, using more illustrations and stories to augment the traditional message style may be appropriate. Similarly, the greater use of drama (skits) and media techniques in the contemporary worship format may convey the message in a way that assures its relevance to and a responsiveness by younger generations. A variation is to have the contemporary service led by an assistant pastor or leader who identifies with the younger generational category. This provides the advantage of a message that is tailored more specifically to the needs of the younger generational group and delivered by a pastor with whom they more closely identify in terms of age and life experience. Having the senior pastor speak at both services has its advantages too, however. It tends to unify the two congregations and dampens the tendency of taking on the aura of two distinct and separate church bodies. The best approach depends upon what the senior pastor is comfortable with, the size of the pastoral staff, and adaptability to some of the considerations outlined above.

Separate worship services are only part of the ministry plan that targets unchurched Boomers or Xers. Equally important is other generationally oriented programming.

Leadership. A major issue under the church-within-a-church approach is staffing. Launching a Boomer or Xer outreach with a separate worship service requires a leader whose time is largely dedicated to this ministry. It also requires a small core of laypersons to get the ministry underway. As the ministry progresses beyond a separate worship service to the establishment of small groups and other generation driven programs, new potential leaders must be recruited and developed from the new congregation. Tim Celek, who left his position as an assistant pastor at a megachurch to plant a new church targeting Generation Xers, emphasizes the importance of not trying to do it all alone. He found that he had to become more like a coach and focus on preparing others in the congregation to use their gifts to carry out the ministry. When the new church, Calvary Church Newport Mesa, changed from a clergy-directed ministry to one focused on developing lay leaders to take on increasing responsibility, the church took a very positive turn, and the ministry grew. Some churches develop several small leadership teams for different aspects of preparing for the worship service. The Xtreme in Plano, Texas, for example, has a drama team, a video team, a music (worship) team, a leadership team, and a programming team.

Dieter Zander, founding pastor of New Song, another church oriented to Generation X, also emphasizes the importance of leader development and the capability of the staff member heading up this new outreach. In the case of Generation Xers, the role of the pastor or staff leader is more that of a mentor or coach. *Inside the Soul of a New Generation* by Celek and Zander provides excellent insight on this aspect of leadership.[4]

Church unity. One of the questions raised concerning the church-within-a-church plan is whether separate services negatively impact the unity and fellowship of the church. Although this is a valid concern, the effect is not much different from having multiple services to accommodate attendance growth. Nor is it conceptually different from the segmentation common in other aspects of ministry such as age-graded Sunday school classes, separate fellowship groups based on age or other common circumstances (i.e., singles, young marrieds, seniors, etc.), and other groups segmented on the basis of common problems, circumstances, or purposes (i.e., men's groups, women's ministries, mutual support or recovery groups, etc.). People gravitate and relate to one another by reason of some common interest or bonding influence, not because they are herded together into a joint worship service.

The fact of separate worship services and other special ministries that are generation specific does not preclude the opportunity for intergenerational interface. Kevin Ford refers to a "generation-skip effect" in many churches. Generation Xers often relate better to their grandparents' generation (Pre-Boomers) than to that of their parents (Boomers). They feel a grandparent-oriented empathy toward Pre-Boomers because of the dedication and commitment they had toward their children, which were generally lacking in the Xers' experience. Generation Xers therefore do not mind mentoring from older generations, from whom they feel they can learn some things their parents did not teach them.[5] The fact that a Caretaker church is sufficiently concerned about younger generations to provide alternative worship and programming agendas to accommodate them also speaks volumes in terms of a genuine Christian interest and concern, especially since "realness" is something that Generation Xers seek. Reaching out to them in their own cultural format can only work in positive ways to break down the generational barriers and open opportunities for fellowship, working together, and the exchange of ideas.

Preplanning. Some of the key elements for a second service that need to be planned for, as emphasized by Arn, include

- *Music.* Music is critical and must reflect the secular preference of the generational category targeted. For younger audiences, this means rhythm, beat, and instrumentation. The size of the instrumental group needed varies with the size of the congregation, but Arn recommends four to five for a congregation of 50 to 100 and five to six for a congregation of 100 to 250. He recommends that music talent be paid in order to provide for better control, accountability, and quality and to maintain a better overall relationship between the musicians and the church.

- *Drama.* Another important tool in Boomer and Xer ministries, drama conveys concepts through illustration, as opposed to description, maintains attention and interest, and augments auditory sense with visual sense for greater retention. Drama of this type generally means skits three to five minutes long that illustrate message-related issues. Using drama requires a good drama coordinator. Professionally prepared scripts are available from several sources, such as Willow Creek. You can obtain their drama catalog by calling 1-800-876-7335.

- *Multimedia.* Younger generations respond to visual and audio communication techniques. These include use of video tapes, overhead projector, audio tapes, film, art, slides, and others. The selection of material used should, of course, reinforce the theme.

- *A planning worship team.* The role of this team or its equivalent is to plan and arrange elements of the worship service (i.e., the sermon, testimonies, audience interaction, etc.) and assure that they fit together into a well-coordinated program. The team schedules rehearsals as necessary to assure such outcome.

- *Promotion.* Effective promotion is a prerequisite to launching a new service. Arn emphasizes the importance of achieving a critical mass, namely, beginning the new service with a sufficient number of people to optimize prospects for sustained success. To satisfy this requirement, the goal should be the greater of fifty people or 35 percent of the present service. A third of these should be unchurched or inactive.

  Effective promotion requires an aggressive campaign that includes personal invitations and public announcements. The latter may include some combination of direct mail, newspaper ads, radio and TV advertising, a telemarketing campaign, and other techniques. Refer to Arn's book mentioned earlier for a detailed discussion on this. One church in the Seattle area launched a new ministry oriented to Generation X through an aggressive door-to-door visitation campaign in which residents were given literature on the new start-up church. Where no one was home, the visitation team members left door-hanger literature describing the new ministry and inviting attendance. This worked extremely well, providing good initial attendance and subsequent growth. So, many avenues exist for getting the word out about the new service, but they all take time and significant effort and funds.[6]

The name. Although the new service is part of an existing church, there is no reason it can't have a new name. The name will greatly influence how it is perceived by the unchurched community you hope to attract. For example, if it's billed as the new contemporary service of the First Baptist Church, it will be perceived as a warmed-over retread of the same old churchianity thinly disguised in order to attract a new crowd. Giving it a different name that stirs the imagination and implies a radical departure from the conventional church format will attract much more interest and curiosity. Here are some of the names used either by postmodern churches or by special postmodern ministries of multigenerational churches: Crosscurrent, Frontline, Xtreme, The Edge, The Forum, The Door, The Flipside, The Glimpse, The Quest, New Song, The Bridge, The Bait Shop, Warehouse 242, The Harbour, AXXESS, New Tribes, Real Life, and New Life. These examples illustrate how names can convey the impression that this group represents something different. Most young people today have a spiritual longing they are seeking to fulfill, but they have rejected the traditional church as being out of date, irrelevant, intolerant, conformist, and consisting of congregations with which they do not "fit" or are not really welcome and in which they will have no influence or say in how things are done. The names above imply a departure from all of these negatives and a format that understands and speaks to their generation.

Apart from a special name for the new contemporary service, but closely related, is the name of the church itself. Denominational labels can be a negative these days. As mentioned earlier, younger generations increasingly shy away from denominational churches and are attracted to those that are nondenominational or at least delete the denominational label from their name. Denominations imply a certain rigidity and inflexibility concerning spiritual truth. The Boomers and Xers tend to be much more open and tolerant toward different interpretations of biblical truth. This does not mean that churches should compromise long-held doctrinal positions; it just means it may be advantageous not to wave a big red flag emphasizing that the church fits into a very rigid belief system that tends to separate it and build walls between other Christ-centered persuasions.

When. Typically, when churches go from one to two services, the Sunday school is sandwiched in between, which provides the opportunity for everyone to attend Sunday school, regardless of which service is attended. The schedule might look like this:

Traditional Service: 8:30 A.M. — 9:30 A.M.
Sunday School: 9:45 A.M. — 10:45 A.M.
Contemporary Service: 11:00 A.M. — 12:00 P.M.

Note that the contemporary service is the second service. This is preferable since it provides the opportunity for a light meal and time of fellowship following the worship service, a feature that can be particularly appealing to younger generations. The meal need not be elaborate. Real Life Church has a time for fellowship and light snacks for those who want to stay after the morning service. Homemade soup, muffins, hot dogs, peanut butter and jelly sandwiches, a taco bar, and a latte bar make up the fare. There is no charge except for the lattes, which cost a dollar. Visitors receive a ticket that entitles them to a free latte.

The other option is to hold the second service at a time other than Sunday morning. If the second service is geared to young Generation Xers, Saturday evening or Sunday evening can work out quite well. The University Presbyterian Church of Seattle, Washington, has two Sunday evening services, both of which are geared to college students. The services are oriented to Generation X in terms of format. This works out well since most of those in attendance are young students without families, making the absence of nursery and children's programs at that time of no consequence. While evening programs generally mean that those who attend do not attend Sunday School, this too is of little consequence because small-group ministries with Bible study and discussion components essentially replace the function performed by Sunday school programs. It is important to avoid the tendency to hold sacrosanct the concept that the Sunday school ministry must be close in time and place to the worship service — or that it must even exist at all. Sunday school is important as a ministry only as long as it fulfills a purpose not otherwise fulfilled or not fulfilled more effectively by another ministry. To consider it otherwise institutionalizes the function so that it exists regardless of whether or not the purpose for which it was originally established remains valid.

Model 3: Two churches in one

This is similar to the church-within-a-church model (model 2) except that the new contemporary ministry is set up on a more autonomous basis as a separate ministry that reports directly to the church board instead of to the senior pastor. Each congregation is led by a pastor who identifies with the target group. Alternatively, the new ministry could report to the senior pastor for broad oversight but still exist under a relatively autonomous charter and be led by a separate pastor. The model bears similarities to planting a new church, but it operates within the confines of an existing church entity and is not designed to split off from the parent entity.

An analogous model in the corporate world would be a company with two decentralized product divisions. *Decentralized* means that most authority to make decisions, as well as management and operating responsibilities, are delegated to the divisions for their respective product lines. The company headquarters retains overall control and approval authority for selected decisions, such as capital expenditures and selection of key divisional management, but for the most part each division is allowed to operate as an independent entity, provided all goes well. In the event that the divisions flounder and do not perform, the parent company intervenes and institutes appropriate management or other changes within the division as necessary.

Figure 10-2 illustrates the organizational concept for model 2 along with two variations for model 3. By remaining in the parent church, the new contemporary arm and the traditional arm share in certain common ministries such as children's, youth, missions, etc. The model also provides opportunities for intergenerational interface and relationships to occur. Other major benefits over two separate churches are the shared facilities, the more efficient utilization of these facilities, and a reduction in other overhead expenses as a percentage of total budget.

From a longer term perspective, the church under model 3 becomes structured to minister effectively in two distinctly different cultural paradigms — one oriented toward the traditional Christian culture, as well as non-Christian seekers who are oriented more toward modernist-era thinking, and the other oriented toward postmodernist cultures. As the societal shift to a postmodernist world increasingly dominates non-Christian moral and social values, the local church is structured to remain relevant. The question might be raised as to what happens if the newer congregation begins to become more dominant. The answer is that it probably reflects a positive outcome in that the church is successfully transitioning to a changing world and a new spiritual challenge.

Figure 10-2

ORGANIZATION CONCEPTS

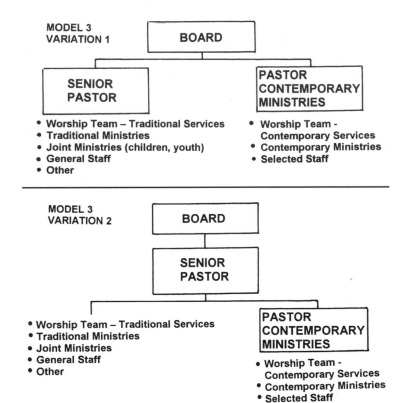

MODEL 2

BOARD

SENIOR PASTOR

- Worship Team – Traditional Services
- Worship Team – Contemporary Services
- Other Ministries
- Staff

MODEL 3 VARIATION 1

BOARD

SENIOR PASTOR

PASTOR CONTEMPORARY MINISTRIES

- Worship Team – Traditional Services
- Traditional Ministries
- Joint Ministries (children, youth)
- General Staff
- Other

- Worship Team - Contemporary Services
- Contemporary Ministries
- Selected Staff

MODEL 3 VARIATION 2

BOARD

SENIOR PASTOR

- Worship Team – Traditional Services
- Traditional Ministries
- Joint Ministries
- General Staff
- Other

PASTOR CONTEMPORARY MINISTRIES

- Worship Team - Contemporary Services
- Contemporary Ministries
- Selected Staff

Many of the necessary considerations regarding model 2 also apply to model 3 — the issues pertaining to church unity, preplanning, name of the ministry, critical mass, and leadership development. More concern about church unity arises under model 3 since the two ministries are more independent of one another. Churches pursuing model 3 are also likely to experience the need for new leadership concepts. Many churches with segmented contemporary ministries increasingly employ a team leadership concept, as opposed to one dominated by a single "point person," as Jordan Cooper describes it. Cooper is teaching pastor at Lakeview Church in Saskatoon, Canada, a church that has initiated a new ministry named The Upper Room. A strong advocate of segmented ministries, Cooper has written a number of articles that can be accessed on the Internet at *www.next-wave.org*.

Model 4: Foster church

A foster home is a household in which a child is given parental care by someone other than its birth or adoptive parent. Similarly, the foster church is one that assists in the nurture and growth of an outside church entity through the use of its premises or physical assets. A Caretaker church may not have the inclination or will to launch a second service, even though it recognizes the need for such an outreach. Many possible reasons could account for the disinclination: an inadequate membership base; insecurity about the concept; lack of will by the church leadership to launch what it perceives as a high-risk undertaking; inadequate congregational interest or enthusiasm for a move too far afield from its ministry comfort zone; a congregation composed disproportionately of older members who feel inadequate in terms of the energy, commitment, and potential lay support required; or possibly a pastor whose ministerial calling is not to a contemporary-style outreach. A fairly strong and well-attended Caretaker church that is concerned for some type of outreach to unchurched younger generations may simply lack what Greg Warner describes as that essential requirement variously termed growth orientation, evangelistic fervor, Great Commission thinking, or apostolic mind-set. The foster church model provides a way that such a church can still participate in a meaningful outreach to unchurched generational groups.

Many Caretaker churches own their property free and clear and have an underutilized church plant in good condition. The concept is to allow an outside group that is prepared to plant a new church targeting unchurched Generation Xers or possibly Boomers to use the church for its meetings at no cost. It represents a meaningful ministry of the host church in that it helps plant a much needed new outreach in the area, while avoiding responsibility for actual implementation.

To assure a harmonious relationship, the new church and the host church must be compatible in terms of basic doctrinal positions. Various options exist concerning the scheduling of services. The new church might meet on either Saturday, or Sunday evening, provided the host church does not have a service on one of those nights. If the church does have such a service but it is not well attended, the church might terminate it and accommodate the new outreach. The new church could also meet on Sunday mornings under a schedule arrangement no different from that described for the segmented worship services of Model 2. Under a close cooperative arrangement, the host might invite the new church to have its children and youth attend its programs for these age groups until the new church develops its own programs.

This concept is really not much different from arrangements under which start-up churches sometimes hold Sunday services in rented or leased Seventh-Day Adventist church facilities. Adventist church facilities can often be leased for use on Sundays since Adventist worship is held on Saturdays. However, the arrangement between the host church and the new church is not a business arrangement, but a ministry. In a sense it is a special type of church planting ministry.

Eventually, of course, as the new church becomes established, it will move out into its own facilities. But it would have received the necessary help during the critical early start-up phase that could well determine success or failure. Once the planted church moves out, the host church has the option of hosting another new start-up church, reverting back to its earlier mode, or perhaps launching a second segmented service on its own. After having observed and, in a sense, participated in such a process through its close cooperation with the start-up church, the host Caretaker church might feel comfortable in launching its own generationally segmented second service. In any case, the venture would likely have interjected a new sense of purpose, vision, and vitality into the church.

Model 5: Church planting

Under conventional church planting, one church "plants" another, targeting a different generational category. As is true for model 4, the major drawback is that it does nothing to posture the mother church for ministries geared to the postmodern cultural paradigm. Nevertheless, church planting can be the optimum approach for some Caretaker, as well as Boomer, churches.

Not all Caretaker churches are small, on the decline, and on the verge of extinction, at least not for the near to intermediate term. As suggested in chapter 3, there will likely be a shakeout and process of consolidation in which weak Caretaker churches phase out as members gravitate toward those that have larger congregations and more to offer in terms of facilities, programs, and preaching. These stronger, surviving Caretaker churches may have flourishing ministries to traditional-Christian-culture congregations. Further, they may already have several services, although not generationally segmented, and may have neither the capacity nor the inclination to disrupt a good thing by adding a generationally targeted new service. At the same time they may recognize the absence of conversion growth in their ministry and the need to address more effectively the evangelism component of their mission statement. The solution and best strategy may therefore be to plant generationally targeted sister churches. This can be true of Boomer-oriented churches, as well.

A good example of successful church planting in the greater Seattle area is Overlake Christian Church, which is currently a large church with an attendance of about five thousand. It is multigenerational in outreach, but most would consider it Boomer oriented. Overlake started planting new churches long before it reached current megachurch status. To date it has planted eight sister churches, all of which have developed into very successful ongoing ministries. Their typical procedure involves selecting a senior pastor for the new church, arranging for facilities in which to meet, providing a nucleus of workers from the parent church to help launch the new ministry, providing initial financial support for a defined period of time, and strongly encouraging members of its congregation who live near the new church location to join and lend their support.

William Easum, consultant on church growth and planting with Easum, Bandy & Associates, emphasizes these key elements in church-planting methodology:

1. Meet in rented facilities. This allows more funds to be directed to people resources, rather than real estate, avoids heavy financial stress, and allows the new church to achieve independence more rapidly.

2. Target a generational category like Boomers or Generation Xers, as opposed to a shotgun strategy.

3. Structure the worship service to the cultural orientation of the target audience.

4. Emphasize small groups and relational evangelism.

5. Emphasize a discipling ministry. Assimilation alone is not enough.

6. Organize a planting team of five to seven highly committed people who are compatible with the target audience. This team, not the charter members, determines the core values of the new outreach and becomes the pastoral team of the church, providing leadership and organizational direction.

7. Keep involvement and commitment, not membership, as the goal. He advocates some type of formal training and hands-on ministry before attendees become members.[7]

The planting team recommended by Easum consists of a team leader (pastor), worship leader, children's minister, shepherd, organizer, re-cruiter, and a financial systems person. The team leader and worship leader should be full-time paid members of the team. The others are part-time and unpaid. The functions of the team leader, worship leader, children's minister, and financial systems person are exactly what they imply. Easum describes the shepherd as one who gives about ten hours per week in providing care for hurting people and organizing support and recovery groups. The organizer is described as a volunteer who designs the ministry systems — a general manager or CEO type. The recruiter, also an unpaid person, helps to organize events that build community relationships.

Churches that do not have the resources or inclination to plant new churches on their own might consider joining with other churches in such a project. This is most feasible by several churches of the same denomination, although this need not be the case assuming reasonable doctrinal compatibility. Joint cooperative projects by like-minded churches offer significant potential in church planting, as well as in other community outreach projects. A good example of the latter is a transitional housing project by several churches for single moms facing abusive relationship or difficult financial circumstances. Such a project was launched recently by ten churches in the Maple Valley, Washington, area that recognized a growing need that each church felt unable to address effectively on its own. The participating churches represent Baptist, Lutheran, Assemblies of God, independent, and other persuasions. They got together, formed a nonprofit corporation, and bought a run-down eight-unit apartment complex, for which each shared equally in the purchase obligation. The complex was renovated largely through volunteer labor and materials provided by the churches, as well as other secular and Christian community groups that wanted to assist in the project. Since the rental rates are structured on a nonprofit, break-even basis, they are quite low. Tenants are sponsored by each of the participating churches, and each church subsidizes the already low rental rate for each tenant it sponsors, based on individual need. Tenants are eligible to remain for one year, during which time each church is involved in helping to rehabilitate the tenants it sponsors through assistance in job training, job referrals, accessing available public programs, and other areas as needed.

Applying the same type of cooperation to church planting would involve establishing a church-planting board made up of representatives from each of the sponsoring churches. This board would be responsible for assembling the planting team along the lines of that described earlier and assisting the team in all necessary arrangements. These include locating suitable facilities, consummating the rental agreement, launching a promotional campaign, establishing a budget, and coordinating with the sponsoring churches. The sponsoring churches each commit to a proportionate share of the budget obligation for a specified period of time, typically one to two years.

A cooperative joint church-planting project of this type requires a pastor who is willing to take the initiative and invite other pastors to explore the possibility. It is probably most effectively presented as a domestic missionary outreach directed toward a large segment of the American postmodern population that is virtually unreachable through the traditional church apart from one of the other strategy models outlined earlier. Assuming these other models are not acceptable to the churches involved, the targeted population segment might logically be viewed as an external (missionary) outreach, rather than as an internal church ministry. To the extent that potential sponsoring churches are missions minded, this perspective should offer appeal, particularly in view of the fact that the United States is now widely regarded as one of the major mission fields of our day. It would also make sense under this line of reasoning to fund the project under the missions budget of each church.

These various alternatives make it clear that the opportunity exists for virtually all churches to participate in today's challenge for expanded outreach to America's growing unchurched population in the new postmodern cultural paradigm. The issue is not really "whether," for those churches that take seriously the Great Commission of Matthew 28:19–20 to make disciples. This charge to the church was given as a command, not an option. The real question is "how." When asked how much effort or cost to incur in solving a client problem, an experienced management consultant once responded, "You've got to cut the cloth to fit the pattern." So it is with churches. The answer to expanded postmodern outreach is to choose among the alternatives described the one that best matches the resources and capabilities of the sponsoring congregation.

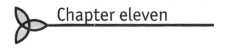

Chapter eleven

UTILIZING THE INTERNET

THE CHURCH IS IN THE INFORMATION BUSINESS — the basic business of communicating the gospel but also communicating to the community that it offers a program that meets the needs of those who are searching for spiritual fulfillment. The Internet is rapidly becoming the predominant communication technology of the twenty-first century. It had 26 million users in 1995 and grew to about 163 million in 1999 according to recent reports — a sixfold increase in four years.[1] That equates to a compound annual growth rate of almost 60 percent. The Barna Research Group concluded from a 1998 survey that 12 percent of the adult population were already using the Internet for religious purposes.[2] George Barna predicts that up to 20 percent of the population will rely to a large degree upon the Internet for its religious input by the year 2010.

The Internet will certainly play a vital and growing role in ministry, particularly to younger members of society. Teenagers are cybersavvy, having grown up with the Net. Older generations are adapting to the new technology, but teens have been immersed in it almost since birth. As a communications medium of choice, the Net is to Generation X what television was to the Boomer generation. Accordingly, churches that do not make this technology a part of their ministry tools will be at a distinct disadvantage. Use of the Internet is particularly important as an implementation element of the strategy models outlined in the preceding chapter. The Net, through church Web sites, represents a primary follow-up source of information for those responding with interest to new ministries being promoted by other means of publicity. Even apart from special promotional campaigns related to launching new generationally segmented ministries, Web sites will increasingly become the means for checking out churches by individuals looking for one that meets their needs.

Internet Web sites have become almost universal among progressive younger churches oriented toward postmodern population segments. Older, more traditional churches have been much slower in taking advantage of this new technology. Church Web sites provide a broad range of information about the church, typically including such items as a brief history of the church, its location, times of worship services, ministry emphasis, and philosophy. Those in search of a church also want information about specific ministries and programs, the pastors and staff, opportunities for involvement, and upcoming special events.

In establishing a Web site, it's a good idea to first decide on its purpose and the intended audience. From an outreach perspective, it should be designed with non-Christian seekers in mind and the particular generational group that is targeted. Exploring the Web sites of other churches on the Net is a good way to get ideas on how to do this effectively. It will also be necessary to find someone to produce and maintain the content, as well as to find a host. The main option with regard to a host is to use a commercial Internet Service Provider (ISP). These companies host Web sites and provide access to the Internet for a modest monthly fee. Finding someone in the congregation who is able to produce the Web page and take over the responsibility for maintaining it is another requirement. This person takes control of what information gets put on the site and ensures that the information remains current.

The cyberchurch

Beyond providing information about the church, the other major application of the Net is as a vehicle for ministry. The so-called cyberchurch or Internet church movement is usually what comes to mind at such mention. Barna envisions a shift from the format of the traditional church to one that is entirely on the Internet as it becomes increasingly integrated into our culture. Others believe this to be an overstatement much along the lines of what was said about radio when it was introduced, along with prognostications that people would stay home from church in favor of radio preachers and churches. Cyberchurches are already on the scene and growing rapidly in numbers, but whether they will actually displace conventional churches to any significant degree remains to be seen.

Many have real concerns concerning cyberchurches. Because of their independence from spiritual accountability, they are an invitation to rampant theological heresy. From a biblical perspective, they are also questionable. For example, they do not meet what many understand as the criteria for corporate worship (Eph. 5:19; Heb. 10:25), mutual support and encouragement (1 Thess. 5:14), bearing one another's burdens (Gal. 6:2), or the administration of church discipline (Matt. 18:15–17; Titus 3:10; 2 Tim. 2:14–18; 2 John 1:11; 1 Cor. 5; 2 Thess. 3:6). However, the issue of cyberchurches is beyond the scope of this book. What is relevant are cyberministries intended to augment and reinforce the basic strategies outlined earlier in expanding outreach to unchurched segments of the population.

Web sites

Web sites represent another means of attracting the unchurched or drawing dropouts back into the fold. In other words, the Internet can be used as an enhancement rather than a replacement. The vehicles for doing this are chat room Bible discussions and interactive Bible studies. Such online interaction has advantages in that people are anonymous and therefore more free to open up in expressing their doubts and concerns. Such online interaction of a religious nature also represents a very new real challenge to the church. The postmodern generation, which is pluralistic in its religious outlook, does not view the Christian faith as "the way, the truth, and the life." Rather, it is one among many religions. However, a genuine spiritual hunger exists, and the church utilizing such cyber-ministries must be one that welcomes questioning and inquiries from those who come from such a mind-set, and be prepared to respond in an effective way. This takes us back to the concepts of narrative and Socratic evangelism discussed in chapter 7 and the requirement for Internet leaders to be qualified in these approaches. To reiterate, the basic objective of such cyber-ministries is to draw inquirers and seekers into the local church where they can be exposed more adequately to the full ministry of the local church.

The full impact of the Internet on church ministries and outreach is a story still being written. But the church needs to be aware of its potential for both good and evil. It is the latest in a succession of revolutionary mass communication changes under the marvels of technology, plowing new advances in the wake of television and radio that preceded it. Like these predecessors it is likely to dramatically open new avenues for communicating the Christian message in increasingly effective ways. Since it is rapidly becoming the primary vehicle for both receiving and sending information, it is imperative that the church learn how to become an active player in this new communications medium and to be in the forefront of exploiting it to maximum advantage.

FINAL THOUGHTS

THE TRADITIONAL CHURCH has always been missions minded. Taking the gospel message to foreign lands and strange cultures has long been regarded as one of the highest callings and priorities of the church. We do not count the cost in terms of time, effort and funds expended in preparing missionaries in terms of studying languages, training for survival, adapting to new environments, and learning the ways of the culture of those to whom they are sent to minister. Nor do we hesitate to establish educational opportunities, build and staff medical facilities, relieve hunger through food programs, and perform a myriad of other local benevolences motivated in part by humanitarian concern but primarily as a means of opening doors to the Christian message. Christian martyrs who have sacrificed their lives in taking the gospel to foreign and often hostile cultures are our greatest heroes, as well they should be. They have not stopped to count the cost in an overriding conviction to fulfill the Great Commission, regardless of the personal sacrifice and risk. And we have come to expect this of them, as well as the church's commitment to support them by all means possible.

But we have an entirely different mind-set when it comes to what we regard as strange new cultures that now reside here in our own country. These "pagan masses" that represent over half of our population speak a different musical language, have no reference point as to right and wrong, and seem to function on an entirely different mental wavelength than those of us who have been reared in solid Christian families and immersed in biblical truth and teaching for most of our lives. While we are willing to fund missionary outposts halfway around the world to reach foreign cultures we do not understand, we are reluctant to structure such outposts in our own backyard to respond to the same challenge domestically.

It is vitally important that the church revise its perception of America from that of a Christian stronghold to that of a growing mission field. A recent *Newsweek* magazine article highlighted the dramatic shift that has taken place in Christianity on a worldwide basis over the past century.[1] At the turn of the twentieth century, about 80 percent of Christians (Catholics and Protestants) were Europeans or North Americans. Today, about 60 percent are African, Asian, or Latin American. *Newsweek* also reports that in Nigeria alone there are seven times as many Anglicans as there are Episcopalians in the United States. And Korea now has four times as many Presbyterians as does America. Former bastions of the Christian faith are becoming mission territories. Evangelists from Latin America and Africa now hold crusades in such countries as Germany and the United Kingdom. Today, India has replaced the United States as the primary source of Jesuit recruits. The decline of the United States as a predominantly Christian nation helps explain the waning number of missionary candidates that mission agencies are experiencing. Woodrow Kroll, in *The Vanishing Ministry,* reported that North American Protestant mission agencies needed to fill four thousand to five thousand openings for full-time missionaries just to keep pace — and even keeping pace constitutes a formula for declining missions outreach in a world of rapid population growth.[2] The situation has undoubtedly deteriorated since the publication of that statistic in 1991.

This background helps put into proper focus the challenge before the Christian church in America today. We live in the very midst of a large and growing mission field — one of the largest in the world. We are no longer a predominately Christian nation where the primary opportunity to propagate the faith lies outside of our national borders. Instead we are a Christian minority in the midst of a predominantly non-Christian culture, not unlike the situation faced by the foreign missionaries we send abroad. Consequently, we need a new perspective and a change in focus that recognizes this reality — a field ripe unto harvest all around us — beckoning the church to recognize and respond to the opportunity. We are well equipped for the challenge and have all that is needed at our disposal to launch a great outreach to the postmodern culture in which we now reside. To do so, however, requires not only a new outreach perspective but a willingness to accept change. We must adopt new ministry methods and formats that respond most effectively to the postmodern cultures targeted in such outreach.

NOTES

Chapter 1. The Generation Driven Trend

1. Neil Howe and Bill Strauss, *13th Gen: Abort, Retry, Ignore, Fail?* (New York: Vintage Books, 1993), 43.

2. Tim Celek and Dieter Zander, *Inside the Soul of a New Generation* (Grand Rapids, Mich.: Zondervan, 1996), 20.

3. *Statistical Abstract of the United States: 1999*, 119th ed. (Washington, D.C.: U.S. Census Bureau, 1999), 16, table 16.

4. George Barna, *The Second Coming of the Church* (Nashville: Word Publishing, 1998), 15-17; George Barna, *The Index of Leading Spiritual Indicators* (Dallas: Word Publishing, 1996), 109.

5. Ibid., 33.

6. "Gallup: U.S. Religious Attitudes Similar to Those of 1947," *Presbyterian News Service*, May 20, 1997; *www.ecunet.org/pcnews/old news/1997/97208.htm.*

7. Barna, *The Index of Leading Spiritual Indicators*, 1-5.

Chapter 2. The Rise of Postmodernism

1. Jimmy Long, *Generating Hope: A Strategy for Reaching the Postmodern Generation* (Downers Grove, Ill.: InterVarsity Press, 1997), 67.

2. Wade Clark Roof, *A Generation of Seekers: The Spiritual Journeys of the Baby Boom Generation* (New York: Harper Collins, 1993), 32-60.

3. Craig Kennet Miller, *Baby Boomer Spirituality* (Nashville: Discipleship Resources, 1993), 33.

4. Roof, *A Generation of Seekers*, 51.

5. Miller, *Baby Boomer Spirituality*, 37.

6. Roof, *A Generation of Seekers*, 51-52, 162-63.

7. Pierre Hegy, "Baby Boomers and the Transmission of Faith" (cover story), *America* 172, no. 3 (February 4, 1995): 5(5).

8. Philip R. Mason, "Ministry in a Postmodern Culture"; *www.ozemail.com.au/~earthtribe.*

9. This copyrighted interview with Michael B. Regele, Kim Hutchins, Dan Allender, and Stuart Hancock was originally published August 9, 1999, in *Mars Hill Review*, a 160-page journal of essays, studies, and reminders of God. For more information, call 800-990-MARS or visit *www.marshillforum.org.*

10. George Barna, *Generation Next: What You Need to Know about Today's Youth* (Ventura, Calif.: Regal books, 1995), 97-106.

Chapter 3. The Caretaker Church — An Endangered Species

1. Bill Hull, *Seven Steps to Transform Your Church* (Grand Rapids, Mich.: Fleming H. Revell, 1993), 167–68.

Chapter 4. About Boomers

1. Wade Clark Roof, *Spiritual Marketplace: Baby Boomers and the Remaking of American Religion* (Princeton, N.J.: Princeton University Press, 1999), 180–216.
2. Wade Clark Roof, *A Generation of Seekers: The Spiritual Journeys of the Baby Boom Generation* (New York: Harper Collins, 1993), 72–73.
3. William Benke and Le Etta Benke, *Church Wake-Up Call: A Ministries Management Approach That Is Purpose-Oriented and Intergenerational in Outreach* (Binghamton, N.Y.: Haworth Press, 2001), 15–16; used with permission.
4. Doug Murren, *The Baby Boomerang* (Ventura, Calif.: Regal Books, 1990), 37–38.
5. Roof, *A Generation of Seekers*, 55–56, 188–89.
6. Wade Clark Roof, "The Baby Boom's Search for God," *American Demographics* 14, no. 12 (December 1992): 50(6).
7. Tom Schaefer, "Worship Changes You, Even If You Don't Feel Changed," Wright-Ridder Newspapers, *Wichita Eagle*, October 18, 1997; *http://texnews.com/religion97tom101897.html.*
8. Roof, *A Generation of Seekers*, 165.

Chapter 5. Reaching Unchurched Boomers

1. D. Sullivan, *American Demographics* 13, no. 1 (October 1991): 42.
2. Rick Warren, *The Purpose Driven Church: Growth without Compromising Your Message and Mission* (Grand Rapids, Mich.: Zondervan, 1995), 46.
3. Doug Murren, *The Baby Boomerang* (Ventura, Calif.: Regal Books, 1990), 36–39.
4. Warren, *The Purpose Driven Church*, 279–92.

Chapter 6. About Generation X (Busters, 13th Generation)

1. Tim Celek and Dieter Zander, *Inside the Soul of a New Generation* (Grand Rapids, Mich.: Zondervan, 1996), 56.
2. Neil Howe and Bill Strauss, *13th Gen: Abort, Retry, Ignore, Fail?* (New York: Vintage Books, 1993), 94–95.
3. William Benke and Le Etta Benke, *Church Wake-Up Call: A Ministries Management Approach That Is Purpose-Oriented and Intergenerational in Outreach* (Binghamton, N.Y.: Haworth Press, 2001), 20–21.
4. Kevin Graham Ford, *Jesus for a New Generation* (Downers Grove, Ill.: InterVarsity Press, 1995), 45–47.
5. Howe and Strauss, *13th Gen: Abort, Retry, Ignore, Fail?*, 36–69, 93–97, 105.
6. Todd Hahn and David Verhaagen, *Reckless Hope: Understanding and Reaching Baby Busters* (Grand Rapids, Mich.: Baker Books, 1996), 29–34.
7. Ford, *Jesus for a New Generation*, 81.

Chapter 7. Reaching Unchurched Generation Xers

1. Lori Leibovich, "A Look inside Fundamentalism's Answer to MTV: The Postmodern Church," *Mother Jones*, July–August 1998, 47.

2. Eric Stanford, "The New Wave of Gen X Churches: Get Your Glimpse of the Future Here," *Next Wave* (December 1999), *www.next-wave.org*.

3. Kevin Graham Ford, *Jesus for a New Generation* (Downers Grove, Ill.: Inter-Varsity Press, 1995), 204–5.

4. Tim Celek and Dieter Zander, *Inside the Soul of a New Generation* (Grand Rapids, Mich.: Zondervan, 1996), 102.

5. Ford, *Jesus for a New Generation*. 228.

6. Celek and Zander, *Inside the Soul of a New Generation*, 126.

7. Ford, *Jesus for a New Generation*, 209.

8. Jimmy Long, *Generating Hope: A Strategy for Reaching the Postmodern Generation* (Downers Grove, Ill.: InterVarsity Press, 1997), 141–52.

9. Todd Hahn and David Verhaagen, *Reckless Hope: Understanding and Reaching Baby Busters* (Grand Rapids, Mich.: Baker Books, 1996), 109.

10. Ford, *Jesus for a New Generation*, 190–91.

11. Andres Tapia, "Reaching the First Post-Christian Generation X," *Christianity Today* 38, no. 10 (September 12, 1994)· 18.

12. A. Allan Martin, "GenXcellent Involvement! Dream Vision Ministries"; see *www.tagnet.org/dvm/index.html*.

Chapter 8. Children and Generation Y (Millennials)

1. William Benke and Milt Bryan, "The World's Most Fruitful Field, Evangelizing," *Today's Child* 14, no. 6 (November–December 1977): 4–6, 44–45. (Warrenton, Mo.: Child Evangelism Fellowship, Inc.).

2. George Barna, *Generation Next: What You Need to Know about Today's Youth* (Ventura, Calif.: Regal Books, 1995), 77–79.

3. Roy B. Zuck and Gene A. Getz, *Christian Youth: An In-Depth Study* (Chicago: Moody Press, 1968).

4. George Barna, *The Index of Leading Spiritual Indicators* (Dallas: Word Publishing, 1996).

5. Barna, *Generation Next*, 77.

6. Ibid., 100–101, 118–19,

7. Mark Tittley, "Ministry and the Millennial Generation," *Next Wave* (May 1999); *www.next-wave.org/may99/millennials.htm*.; Hazel Reinhart, "Generation Y Finding Values in Cub Scouts," *Spokesman Review*, October 31, 1999, 9; Wendy Harns, "Generation Y2/OK Class of '00 Confidently Marches into Bright Future," *Spokesman Review*, May 25, 2000, A1; Wendy Murray Zoba, "Generation Y Papers, Defining Generation Y, the Next Generation," *Youthwork Magazine* (May 1997); Karen Vella-Zarb, "Meet the Future: Its Your Kids," *Fortune*, July 24, 2000, 144; Graeme Codrington, "Twelve Sentences That Define Generation Y," *The Edge Consulting* (August 1999); *www.youth.co.za/resource003.htm*; Graeme Codrington, "The Difference between

Generation X and Generation Y," *The Edge,* issue 6a + b; *www.ngkerdrc.co.za/jeug/ generasie.html;* "The Millennial Generation, Hope Unlimited and Sidewalk Sunday School International"; *www.sidewalksundayschool.org/pages/millennial _ 1.htm.*

Chapter 9. Preparing for Change

1. Bill Hull, *Seven Steps to Transform Your Church* (Grand Rapids, Mich.: Fleming H. Revell, 1993), 167–68.
2. Rick Warren, *The Purpose Driven Church: Growth without Compromising Your Message and Mission* (Grand Rapids, Mich.: Zondervan, 1995), 251–77.
3. William Benke and Le Etta Benke, *Church Wake-Up Call: A Ministries Management Approach That Is Purpose-Oriented and Intergenerational in Outreach* (Binghamton, N.Y.: Haworth Press, 2001).
4. Charles Arn, *How to Start a New Service* (Grand Rapids, Mich.: Baker Books, 1997), 16.
5. Ibid., 20.
6. Ibid., 19.
7. Warren, *The Purpose Driven Church,* 245.

Chapter 10. Alternative Outreach Models

1. Greg Warner, "Multicongregational Churches Becoming Trend in U.S. Worship, Biblical Recorder," *Journal of the Baptist State Convention of Georgia* (July 30, 1999); *www.biblicalrecorder.org/news/7_30 _ 99/9/multicongregational.html.*
2. Charles Arn, *How to Start a New Service* (Grand Rapids, Mich.: Baker Books, 1997), 14, 17, 23, 24.
3. Larry Gilbert, *How to Influence Your Loved Ones for Christ When You Don't Have the Gift of Evangelism* (Elkton, Md.: Church Growth Institute; printed by Morris Publishing, Kearney, Neb., 2001), 7.
4. Tim Celek and Dieter Zander, *Inside the Soul of a New Generation* (Grand Rapids, Mich.: Zondervan, 1996), 143–59.
5. Kevin Graham Ford, *Jesus for a New Generation* (Downers Grove, Ill.: InterVarsity Press, 1995), 207.
6. Arn, *How to Start a New Service,* 153–80.
7. William Easum, excerpt from the *Easum Report,* Easum, Bandy & Associates; *www.easum.com/church.htm.*

Chapter 11. Utilizing the Internet

1. Steven Lottering, "The Emerging Mission Field: Cyber-Space and Beyond," *The Edge,* issue 1 (winter 2000); *www.youth.co.za/theedge/issue01/issue1-04.htm.*
2. George Barna, *The Second Coming of the Church* (Nashville: Word Publishing, 1998).

Epilogue. Final Thoughts

1. Kenneth Woodward, "The Changing Face of the Church," *Newsweek* (April 16, 2001): 48–51.

2. Woodrow Kroll, *The Vanishing Ministry* (Grand Rapids, Mich.: Kregel Publications, 1991), 105.

Other books from The Pilgrim Press

BEHOLD I DO A NEW THING
Transforming Communities of Faith
C. Kirk Hadaway

Recent talk and thinking about congregations concentrate on declining church attendance. Author Kirk Hadaway thinks an important part of the conversation is missing — how can churches, in spite of the decline, remain engaged in the mission of transforming lives? Looking at churches in new ways and holding new expectations will allow church leadership to guide congregations in the journey where transformation and renewal are constant and embraced.

ISBN 0-8298-1430-2 / paper / 160 pages / $15.00

HOW TO GET ALONG WITH YOUR CHURCH
Creating Cultural Capital for Ministry
George B. Thompson Jr.

This resource incorporates Thompson's research and observations on pastoring a church. He finds that the pastors who are most successful in engaging their parishioners are the ones who develop "cultural capital" within their congregations, meaning that they invest themselves deeply into how their church does its work and ministries.

ISBN 0-8298-1437-X / paper / 176 pages / $17.00

FUTURING YOUR CHURCH
Finding Your Vision and Making It Work
George B. Thompson Jr.

This resource allows church leaders to explore their congregation's heritage, its current context, and its theological bearings. Dr. Thompson provides insights that enable church members to discern what God is currently calling the church to do in this time and place. It is a practical, helpful tool for futuring ministry.

ISBN 0-8298-1331-4 / paper / 128 pages / $14.95

THE BIG SMALL CHURCH BOOK
David R. Ray

Over sixty percent of churches have fewer than seventy-five people in attendance each Sunday. *The Big Small Church Book* contains information on everything from practical business matters to spiritual development. Clergy and lay leaders of big churches can learn much here as well.

ISBN 0-8298-0936-8 / paper / 256 pages / $15.95

LEGAL GUIDE FOR DAY-TO-DAY CHURCH MATTERS
A Handbook for Pastors and Church Leaders
Cynthia S. Mazur and Ronald K. Bullis

This book belongs on every pastor's desk because the church is not exempt from the growing number of lawsuits filed each year. The authors are clergy as well as attorneys.

ISBN 0-8298-0990-2 / paper / 148 pages / $6.95

To order these or any other books from
The Pilgrim Press call or write to:

**The Pilgrim Press
700 Prospect Avenue East
Cleveland, Ohio 44115-1100**

Phone orders: 1-800-537-3394 • Fax orders: 216-736-2206

Please include shipping charges of $4.00 for the first book and $0.75 for each additional book.

Or order from our web sites at
www.pilgrimpress.com and *www.ucpress.com*.

Prices subject to change without notice.